Book of Evidences

The Miracles of the Prophet

(Peace and Blessings be Upon Him)

Ibn Katheer

Copyright

Ibn Katheer

Editor

Imam Ahamd

Table of Comtents

i

ii

v

vii

ix

x

xi

Translator's note

Praise be to Allah the Exalted, Lord of the Universe and our beloved Prophet (P.B.U.H.) and his family, companions and those who followed their rightly guided ways till Judgement Day.

The Miracles of the Prophet is an outstanding book of *Al-Muhadith* Ibn Katheer which deals with the miracles performed by the Prophet over the twenty three years of prophecy. We thank Allah for the success He granted us, of which if it were not for him, this work could not have been possible. We have translated this book using very simple English. Since Arabic is a very rich and vast language, it makes very difficult to translate. Because of this, We were forced during the process of translation, We were forced to add, delete, elaborate and translate by meaning so as to make it possible for the English reader to understand and at the same time, we made sure that we preserved and never distorted the author's

1

thoughts and ideas he intended to pass to the readers.

The Author's Biography

In the name of Allah The Most Gracious The Most Merciful.

His Name and Lineage

He is Al-Hafidh Al-Kabeer Ahmad Ad-Din Ismail Ibn Omar Ibn Kathi'r Ibn Thau Ibn Daara Al-Qurashi Al-Basr then Damascus Shafi' scholar.

His Birth

He was born, may Allah Bless him in a village in Busra in Syria, in the year of 701H – 1303AD.

His Quest for Knowledge

After the death of his father, Al-Hafidh Ibn Kathi'r traveled together with his brother to Syria

2

during the year 707H, and like what the author of the book of *Shatharat Al-Dhahab* said, he memorized the Tan'bii and displayed it in the year 718H and also memorized Al-*Mukhtasar Ibn Al-Haajib* and studied from Al-Burhan Al-Fajani and Al-Kamal Ibn Shaaban and he accompanied Ibn Taymiyyah and Al-Kaamil and studied jurisprudence at Al-Ashlihan. He wrote during his early age the judgment of the book of Tan'bii. He had a strong memory and fine understanding.

Ibn Hajar said: "He was the representative of the science of Hadith among the scholars of jurisprudence and during his lifetime, he authored books which benefited people even after his death. He accompanied Al-Mizii and benefited from his knowledge and later, married his daughter. He was also a student of Sheikh Taqi Din Ibn Taymiyyah.

Ibn Habib quoted about him and said; He was an Imam, narrator, leader in fighting falsehood, he gathered knowledge and authored

3

many books and issued religious decrees which spread over regions. He rose to be among the most prominent scholars specialized in the science of hadith ,history and exegesis (tafsir)

His written work

The major written works of Al-Hafidh Ibn Kathir are as follows:

❖ Al-Bidayah Wa Al-Nihaya

❖ Tafsir Al-Qur'an Al-Karim

❖ Al-Ijtihad Fi Twajab Al-Jihad

❖ Jaami' Al-Masanid

❖ Mukhtasar Ulum Al-Hadith

Ikhtisar Al-Sirat Al-Nabi, priinted as Al-Fusul Fi Ikhtisar Siraat Al-Nabi

❖ Tabakat Shafi'

❖ Commentaries of Sahih Al-Bukhari

His Death

He died in the month of Sha'aban the year 774H – 1373AD in Damascus and buried at the cemetery of Al-Sufiyah beside Ibn Taymiyyah. May Allah have mercy on Al-Hafidh Ibn Katheer.

Significative evidences

The Qur'an Karim

Among the significative evidences is the Holy Qur'an which was revealed to the Prophet (P.B.U.H.) which is the greatest miracle. Allah the Exalted dared mankind and jinn to team up and produce a like thereof by saying in His Holy Book:

"If the mankind and the jinn were to come together to produce the kind of this Qur'an, they could not produce the like thereof, even if they helped one another"

And Allah the Exalted also says:

"And this Qur'an is not such as could ever be produced by other than Allah (Lord of the heavens and the earth) but it is a confirmation of (the revelation) which was before it [i.e. the

6

Taurat (Torah), and the Injeel (Gospel)], and a full explanation of the Book (i.e. laws decreed for mankind) – wherein there is no doubt – from the Lord of the 'Alamin (mankind, jinn, and all that exists).

Or do they say: "He (Muhammad PBUH) has forged it?) Say: "Bring then a Surah (chapter) like unto it, and call upon whomsoever you can besides Allah, if you are truthful!.

Nay, they have belied the knowledge whereof they could not comprehend and what has not yet been fulfilled (i.e. their punishment). Thus those before them did belie. Then see what was the end of the Zalimun (polytheists and wrong-doers)!"

Allah the Exalted says in His Holy Book that all the creatures have tried in challenging the Holy Qur'an like what He says:

"But if you do it not, and you can never do it then fear the Fire (Hell) whose fuel is men and stones, prepared for the disbelievers."

The Qur'an informs about the past

The Holy Qur'an talks about the past truthfully and mentions what was revealed in the books of the Christians and the Jews, despite the fact that it was revealed to an unlettered man who knew not how to write. Allah The Exalted says:

"And you (O Muhammad) were not at the side of the Tur (Mount) when We did call: [it is said that Allah called the followers of Muhammad PBUH and they answered His call, or that Allah called Musa (Moses). But (you are sent) as a mercy from your Lord, to give warning to a people to whom no warner had come before you: in order that they may remember or receive admonition. [Tafsir At-Tabari]
وَمَا كُنتَ بِجَانِبِ ٱلطُّورِ إِذْ نَادَيْنَا وَلَٰكِن رَّحْمَةً مِّن رَّبِّكَ لِتُنذِرَ قَوْمًا مَّآ أَتَىٰهُم مِّن نَّذِيرٍ مِّن قَبْلِكَ لَعَلَّهُمْ يَتَذَكَّرُونَ ۝

8

ذَٰلِكَ مِنْ أَنۢبَآءِ ٱلْغَيْبِ نُوحِيهِ إِلَيْكَ ۚ وَمَا كُنتَ لَدَيْهِمْ إِذْ يُلْقُونَ

أَقْلَٰمَهُمْ أَيُّهُمْ يَكْفُلُ مَرْيَمَ وَمَا كُنتَ لَدَيْهِمْ إِذْ

يَخْتَصِمُونَ ﴿٤٤﴾

Allah The Exalted also says:

"This is a part of the news of the *Ghaib*
(unseen, i.e. the news of the past nations of
which you have no knowledge) which we
reveal to you (O Muhammad). You were not
with them, when they cast lots with their
pens as to which of them should be charged
with the care of Maryam (Mary) nor were
you with them when they disputed."

And Allah the Exalted says in Suratul Yusuf

"That is the news of the *Ghaib* (Unseen)
which We reveal to you (O Muhammad).
You were not (present) with them when they
arranged their plan together, and (while)
they were plotting."

"And most of mankind will not believe even
if you desire it eagerly."

"And no reward you (O Muhammad) ask of

9

لَقَدْ كَانَ فِى قَصَصِهِمْ عِبْرَةٌ لِّأُوْلِى ٱلْأَلْبَٰبِ مَا كَانَ حَدِيثًا يُفْتَرَىٰ وَلَٰكِن تَصْدِيقَ ٱلَّذِى بَيْنَ يَدَيْهِ وَتَفْصِيلَ كُلِّ شَىْءٍ وَهُدًى وَرَحْمَةً لِّقَوْمٍ يُؤْمِنُونَ ۝

them (those who deny your Prophethood) for it (The Qur'an) is no less than a Reminder and an advice unto the *Alamin* (men and jinn)."

To the end of the Surah saying:

"Indeed in their stories, there is a lesson for men of understanding. It (the Qur'an) is not a forged statement but a confirmation of Allah's existing Books) which were before it [i.e. the *Taurat* (Torah), the *Injeel* (Gospel) and other Scriptures of Allah] and a detailed explanation of everything and a guide and a Mercy for the people who believe."

The Qur'an informs what will happen in the Future

The Holy Qur'an foretells what will happen in the future, so does the Traditions of the Prophet together as I have mentioned in the book

10

of Tafsir (Tafsir Ibn Kathir). Allah The Exalted says:

"Verily, your Lord knows that you do stand (pray at night) a little less than two thirds of the night, or half the night, or a third of the night, and also a party of those with you. And Allah measures the night and the day. He knows that you are unable to pray the whole night, so He has turned to you (in mercy). So, recite you of the Qur'an as much as may be easy for you. He knows that there will be some among you sick, others traveling through the land seeking of Allah's Bounty, yet others fighting in Allah's Cause. So recite as much of the Qur'an as may be easy (for you), and perform As-Salat (Iqamat-as-Salat) and give Zakat, and lend to Allah a goodly loan. And whatever good you send before you for yourselves (i.e. Nawafil non-obligatory acts of worship: prayers, charity, fasting, Hajj and 'Umrah), you will

11

certainly find it with Allah, better and greater in reward. And seek forgiveness of Allah. Verily, Allah of Oft-Forgiving, Most-Merciful."

This surah is among the first one's revealed in Mecca and also Suratul Iktaraba. **Allah The Exalted says:**

"Their Multitude will be put to flight, and they will show their backs. Nay, but the Hour is their appointed time (for their full recompense), and the Hour will be more grievous and more bitter."

The Qur'an and its Just Laws

The Qur'an contains Just Laws, which enjoin people to do good and forbid from evil. It becomes clear to any understanding and intelligent person who puts them into consideratithat they have been revealed by One knowledgeable of the unseen, merciful to His servants. **Allah The Exalted says:**

"And the word of your Lord has been fulfilled in truth and in justice. None can change his words. And he is The All-Hearer, The All-Knower"

Allah says:

"Alif-Lam-Ra [These letters are one of the miracles of the Qur'an and none but Allah (Alone) knows their meanings]. (This is) a Book, the Verses whereof are perfected (in every sphere of knowledge), and then explained in detail from One (Allah) Who is All-Wise Well-Acquainted (with all things)."

Allah The Exalted says:

"He it is Who has sent his Messenger

13

(Muhammad Allah's peace and blessing be upon Him) with guidance and the religion of truth (Islam) that He may make it (Islam) superior to all religions. And All-Sufficient is Allah as a Witness."

Refutation of the creation The Qur'an

The *Mutakalimin* (some Muslim theologians) claim that the Holy Quran is not the spoken words of Allah but part of His creation. This belief is blasphemous since the Qur'an is not a creation but Allah's spoken Words revealed to His Prophet (P.B.U.H.).

The Qur'an as a clear evidence of Allah's message till the Judgement Day

The Qur'an, which was conveyed by the Prophet (P.B.U.H.), has a peculiar style which differs from the Prophet's (P.B.U.H.) speech. Similarly, the Prophet's (P.B.U.H.) speech preserved as His Traditions, has a peculiar style

14

which not even His companions or those who came after them can imitate. Imam Ahmad relates that Abu Hurairah (R.A.) said he heard the Prophet (P.B.U.H.) saying, "No prophet was sent but was given signs by which people would believe in him. Surely, what I have been given is a revelation (Qur'an) and I hope to have the most followers on The Day of Judgment."

The Prophet's (P.B.U.H.) characteristics and behavior

Among the significative evidence is the Prophet's immaculate behavior and character, his perfect physical composition, courage, gentleness, generosity, asceticism, contentment, beautiful companionship, honesty, piety, nobility and his good upbringing.

On this issue best is what our Sheikh Abu Al-Abbass Ibn Taymiyyah mentioned in his book, responding to those Christians and Jews who falsified the Prophet (P.B.U.H.). He said, "his biography is a sign of Prophethood, so are the laws that he came with, his followers and the knowledge they had is also a sign, so is their piety and faithfulness and the miracles worked by saints is also among the signs of his Prophethood."

Infallibility of the Prophet (P.B.U.H.)

The Prophet's (P.B.U.H.) knowledge defies ignorance and his perfect religion defies the claims that it is his innovation. These two facts affirm that he was veracious, sincere and genuine and was aware of that.

Allah The Exalted says:

"By the star when it goes down (or vanishes). Your companion (Muhammad SAW) has neither gone astray nor has erred. Nor does he speak of (his own) desire. It is only a revelation revealed."

"Verily, this is the Word (this Qur'an brought by) a most honorable messenger [Jibril (Gabriel), from Allah to Prophet Muhammad].

Owner of power, (and high rank) with (Allah), Lord of the Throne.

Obeyed (by the angels in the heavens) and trustworthy.

And (O people) your companion (Muhammad SAW) is not a mad man.

And indeed he (Muhammad SAW) saw him [Jibril (Gabriel)] in the clear horizon (towards the east).

And he (Muhammad SAW) withholds not a knowledge of the Unseen.

And it (the Qur'an) is not the word of the outcast Shaitan (Satan).

Then where are your going?

Verily, this (the Qur'an) is no less than a reminder to (all) the *Alamin* (mankind and jinn)).

To whomsoever among you who wills to walk straight.

$$\text{وَإِنَّهُۥ لَتَنزِيلُ رَبِّ ٱلۡعَـٰلَمِينَ} \ (١٩٢)$$

And you cannot will unless (it be) that Allah wills – the Lord of the *Alamin* (mankind, jinn and all that exists).

Allah the Exalted says:

"And truly, this (the Qur'an) is a revelation from the Lord of the *Alamin* (mankind, jinn and all that exists). Which the trustworthy *Ruh* [Jibril (Gabriel)] has brought down. Upon your heart (O Muhammad SAW) that you may be (one) of the warners, In the plain Arabic language."

And Allah The Exalted says:

"Neither would it suit them nor they can (produce it). Verily, they have been removed far from hearing it. So invoke not with Allah another *ilah* (God) lest you should be among those who receive punishment."

$$\text{وَمَا يَنۢبَغِى لَهُمۡ وَمَا يَسۡتَطِيعُونَ} \ (٢١١)$$

Visual Evidence of His Prophet hood

In this chapter, Al-Hafidh Ibn Katheer (R.A.) explains tangible heavenly and earthly evidences.

The Heavenly Miracles

Cleavage of the Moon

He said (Ibn Kathir), the most miraculous of all is the cleavage of the moon. Allah The Allah Exalted says:

"The Hour has drawn near, and the moon has been cleft asunder (the people of Mecca requested the Prophet Muhammad (P.B.U.H.) to show them a miracle so he showed them the splitting of the moon). And if they see a sign, they turn away and say: 'This is continuous magic'. They belied the verses of Allah – this (Qur'an) and followed their own lusts. And every matter will be settled (according to the kind of deeds: goods deeds will take their doers to Paradise,

19

and similarly evil deeds will take their doers to Hell). And indeed there has come to them news (in this Qur'an) where in there is (enough warning) to check (them from evil), perfect wisdom (this Qur'an), but (the preaching of) warners benefit them not."·

All the scholars have agreed upon that the cleavage of the moon occurred during the time of the Prophet (P.B.U.H.). There are many Prophetic traditions that support and substantiate that for example.

The version of Anas Ibn Malik:

Imam Ahmad relates that Anas said: The people of Mecca asked the Prophet (P.B.U.H.) to show them a miracle, so he split the moon into two. Allah The Exalted says:

"The Hour has drawn near, and the moon has been cleft asunder (the people of Mecca requested the Prophet Muhammad SAW to show them a miracle so he showed them the splitting of the moon). "

Imam Al-Bukhari relates that Anas Ibn Malik said: The people of Mecca asked the Messenger of Allah to show them a miracle, he therefore cleft the moon, the two pieces were seen on the opposite sides of Mount Hira.

The Version of Abdullahi Ibn Abbas:

Imam Al-Bukhari relates that, Abdullahi Ibn Abbas said: The cleavage of the moon occurred during the time of the Prophet (P.B.U.H.)

The Version of Abdullahi Ibn Umar Ibn Khattab:

Abdullahi Ibn Umar said: Allah The Exalted says:

"The Hour has drawn near, and the moon has been cleft asunder (the people of Mecca requested the Prophet Muhammad (P.B.U.H.) to show them a miracle so he showed them the splitting of the moon). "

This occurred during the time of the Prophet (P.B.U.H.), the moon split into two, a piece in front of the mountain and another behind it then the Prophet (P.B.U.H.) said: "O Lord bear witness ".

The Version of Abdullahi Ibn Mas'ood:

Imam Ahmad relates that Ibn Mas'ood said: The moon split into two during the time of the Prophet (P.B.U.H.) while we were watching, then Prophet (P.B.U.H.) said, "Bear witness "

And Ibn Jarir narrated that, Ibn Sirin said: I was told that Ibn Mas'ood used to say that the moon was cleaved.

How did the cleavage of the moon occur while it was never seen in the other parts of the world?

Some of the stories say that, the moon entered the Prophet's (P.B.U.H.) pocket and come out from his sleeves, but such stories have no origin.

The moon was split into two in the sky. One piece went behind mount Hira and the other one went to it's other side, leaving the mountain in between, while the people of Mecca were watching. Most of the people thought it was magic. So when those who were traveling reached Mecca, they were asked about the moon issue and they narrated what they saw, from then on it became clear to the people of Mecca that the cleavage of the moon was genuine, real and true.

If you were asked:

Why was this not known all over the world ?

The answer is:

Who disagrees? ...The disbelievers have never believed in any miracles before. Most of them witnessed this miracle and others heard about it but they might have never talked of its occurrence because by doing so they would have acknowledged his Prophethood, or they pretendedto forget, as though it never happened. On the contrary many travelers have talked of the temple in India which has inscriptions on it, that it was built the day the moon was cleft.

The fact that the cleaving occurred at night, most people might not have witnessed it, because they were asleep. And Allah The Exalted knows best.

24

The Prophet's (P.B.U.H.) prayer for rain

As far as the heavenly miracles are concerned, the Prophet prayed for rain for his people when it delayed, his prayer was answered so fast that, it started raining before he descended the pulpit.

In another version: Imam Al-Bukhari relates that Anas Ibn Malik said: A man entered the mosque on the day of Jumuah (Friday prayers) through the door that faces the Prophet (P.B.U.H.) while he was on the pulpit preaching and said:

O Messenger of Allah, my animals have perished and means have been exhausted, so ask Allah for rain. Then the Prophet (P.B.U.H.) raised his hands and said,

"O Allah make it rain (thrice)". Anas said:

"I swear by Allah, there were no clouds in the sky

25

not even a single one of them. Then suddenly, a thick heavy cloud covered us and it rained, we never saw the sky for a week. Then a man entered from the same door in the following Jumuah (Friday) while the prophet was preaching and said: "O Messenger of Allah, ask Allah to stop the rain. Then, the Prophet (P.B.U.H.) raised his hands, prayed and the rain stopped".

And in another version Imam Al-Buhkari reports from Anas Ibn Malik that Umar Ibn Khattab said: O Allah we used to asking you to make it rain through the intermediary of Prophet (P.B.U.H.) and you made it rain, so we are asking you to make it rain through the intermediary of the Prophet's uncle".

Earthly Miracles

The earthly miracles occurred on both living things and non-living things.

Earthly miracles on Non-Living things

Water Springing out of the Prophet's (P.B.U.H.) fingers

Imam Al-Bukhari relates that Anas Ibn Malik said: I saw the Messenger of Allah while it was time for Asr prayers, people wanted to perform ablution, water was not to be found. A utensil with water was brought to the Messenger of Allah, he placed his hand in it and told the people to come and perform ablution. I saw water springing out of his fingers. Everyone performed ablution. The hadith has also been reported by Imam Muslim, Imam Al- Tirmidhy and Imam Al-Nisai.

And in another version Imam Ahmad relates that Anas Ibn Malik said: The Prophet (P.B.U.H.) went out as usual with some of his companions. Then when it was time for prayers, they couldn't find where to make ablution. They said:

O Messenger of Allah we cannot find water. A man came went and came back with a bucket which has little water in it, the Prophet (P.B.U.H.) made ablution, then he straightened his four fingers towards the bucket (water sprung out of them) and said come and make ablution. Al-Hassan said: Anas was questioned:

how many were they? He said: seventy or more. This hadith was also reported by Imam Al-Bukhari

In Another version Imam Ahmad relates that Anas said: The Prophet (P.B.U.H.) and some of his companions were in Al-Zura'a. A utensil with water was brought to him, he placed his wrists in the water then water sprung from the tips of his fingers and between them, and all of them made ablution. I asked Anas, "how many were you?" He said we were three hundred. Imam Muslim also reported this hadith in the same manner.

Springing of water from the well of Hudaibiya

Imam Al-Bukhari relates that, Al-Bara'a Ibn Hazib said: During the day of Hudaibiya we were one thousand and four hundred. Hudaibiya is a well, we crowded it and drunk from it, until there was no water left. The Prophet (P.B.U.H.) sat next to the well, asked for water and rinsed his mouth then spat inside the well (water sprung from the well). We camped close to it and drunk until we got satisfied and so did our animals.

The moving of the tree towards the Prophet and covering him

Imam Muslim relates that, Jabir Ibn Abdullah said in a long hadith: We traveled with the Messenger of Allah until we came down a wide valley. The Messenger of Allah went to relieve himself so I followed him carrying a container of water. He had nothing to cover himself with, only two trees which were beside the valley. He went towards one of them and bent some of its branches and said, "through Allah The Exalted move towards me." They moved until they covered him. Jabir said: I kept watching until I feared the Prophet (P.B.U.H.) could hear me so I sat waiting; fortunately enough, he came and the trees dispersed. He asked me "did you see my place?", I replied, "yes I saw"....

The increasing and springing of water in the presence of Prophet (P.B.U.H.) in his conquests and journeys

We heard the food which the Prophet (P.B.U.H.) was holding supplicating Allah The Exalted

Imam Al-Bukhari relates that, Abdullah ibn

Mas'ood said: We were with the Prophet (P.B.U.H.) traveling, our water supplies went short, then he said, "send for a container with some water". They brought a container with a little water in it, he then put his hands in it and said, "life is on blessed purity and blessing are from Allah The Exalted." He (Ibn Mas'ood) said:

I saw water spring out of the Prophet's (P.B.U.H.) fingers and we used to hear the food which the Prophet (P.B.U.H.) ate supplicating Allah The Exalted.

The hadith of Imran Ibn Huswain

In the version of Imran Ibn Huswain: Imam Al-Bukhari and Imam Muslim relates that Imran Ibn Hussein said: We were with the Prophet (P.B.U.H.) on a journey, then the night fell, we all slept until we were awoken by the heat of the sun, the first one to wake up among us was Abu Bakar and we never used to wake the Prophet

(P.B.U.H.) until he did so himself. Then Umar woke up and stood next to the Prophet (P.B.U.H.) and he raised his loud voice saying, "*Takbir!*" until the Prophet woke up and ordered us continue with the journey. We traveled till the sun was sky high, he dismounted, and led us in prayer, one of the companions did not join us in prayer. When he finished praying, he asked him, "what stopped you from praying with us?"

He said: O Messenger of Allah I had a wet dream.

He commanded him to do *tayammum* and pray. We kept looking for water due to thirst, then we met a woman and asked her where we can find water. She replied there is no water for us. We then asked her the distance between her people and water? She said the distance is a day and night away. We took her to the Prophet (P.B.U.H.) and she told him what she told us and that she has two orphans; her husband died. The Prophet (P.B.U.H.) asked for her camel that was carrying water, then he took the container

32

carrying water and placed its opening on his mouth and drunk. He then sent it to us – forty thirsty people – we all drunk from it until we were all satisfied and filled our leather water-bags. The man among us who had a wet dream took a bath, our animals could hardly walk from the weight of the water we were carrying. The Prophet (P.B.U.H.) then ordered us to gather some bread and dates for the lady and he then handed them to her and said, "Take this and feed your family with it and know that we have not reduced from your water". When she reached home, she informed her people that she had met the best of all sorcerers, or a Prophet as they claimed. She later became a Muslim along with her family.

Increment of water flow of a spring in Tabuk

Imam Muslim relates that Muadh Ibn Jabal said: We went out with the Prophet (P.B.U.H.) in

Maghrib and *Isha* together. He then said: "In deed, tomorrow you shall come across the spring of Tabuk, do not approach it till the light of day appears, and he who is going to approach it among you should not touch its water until I come". When we reached, two men had already approached it before us, and there was a spring with little water. The Prophet asked them whether they touched it, they said they had. Then Prophet (P.B.U.H.) scolded them for that. The two then gathered sand around the spring. The Prophet (P.B.U.H.) washed his hands and face in the springand its water gushed out with force and all the people drunk from its water. The Prophet (P.B.U.H.) told Muaadh, "If you live long, you will see the place full of water."

The Prophet's abundance of provision

The increment of milk of the people of Al-Sufaa

Imam Ahmad relates that Abu Huraira was saying, "I swear to Allah The Exalted, I sometimes was not able to stand because of hunger. One day, I sat down by the road which was used by most people, then Abu Bakar passed and I asked him about a verse in the Qur'an Karim. I only asked, so that he invites me but he never did. Then Umar passed and I asked him about a verse in the Qur'an. I only asked, so that he invites me, but he did not. Then Abu Qassim – the Prophet (P.B.U.H.) passed, he knew by the look on face, he called "O Abu Huraira !,"

I said: Here I am O Messenger of Allah.

He said: "The truth", I asked for his permission (to follow him) and he accepted. I followed him and we found a bowl of milk.

He asked, "Where is this milk from?"

35

They said: It is a present from so and so, the family of so and so.

He called, "Abu Huraira"

I said: Here I am O Messenger of Allah.

The Prophet said, "Go to the people of Al-Sufaa and call them".

Abu Huraira explained that: the people of Al-Sufaa were guests of Islam, they did not have any relatives nor property. Whenever the Prophet received any present, he sent to them part of it.

Abu Huraira said: Calling of the people of Al-Sufaa made me sad because I wanted to take a drink from the milk that would strengthen me for the rest of my day and night. The milk was not enough for all of us but I had to obey Allah and His Messenger.

They came and the Prophet asked them to sit down and ordered me to serve them. A man would drink until he is satisfied and then I pass it to another and he also drinks until he is satisfied. I continued this, until I served the last one of them. I then gave it to the Messenger of Allah. He took the bowl with a little milk in it and placed it in his hands, then raised his head and smiled and said, "We are the only two remaining (not having drunk)".

I said, "That is true". Then the Prophet (P.B.U.H.) told me to sit down and drink. I sat down and drunk and he kept telling me to drink. I proceeded drinking until I told him I could not drink any more. I gave him back the bowl and he drunk what was remaining.[34]

Ummu Malik's Ghee

Imam Muslim relates that, Jabir said that Umm Malik used to always give the Prophet (P.B.U.H.) ghee as a present. Her sons used to come and ask her for something to eat bread with, she never used to find anything other than the ghee she usually presents to the Prophet (P.B.U.H.) (which never got finished).

So that day she checked and estimated how much of ghee was left; from then on, it decreased as she used it. Later she went to the Prophet and informed him what happened.

He (P.B.U.H.) said to her, "If you had left it without checking its quantity, you would have always been having ghee".

In another version, Imam Muslim relates that Jabir said: A man came to the Prophet (P.B.U.H.) asking for food, so he gave him a certain quantity of barley. They continued eating from the barley, him, his wife and their guests till the day he weighed what was remaining. He then went and told the Prophet (P.B.U.H.).

The Prophet said to him, "If you had not weighed it, you would have still been eating from it".

The Prophet's (P.B.U.H.) miracle of increasing food

Imam Al-Bukhari relates that Anas Ibn Malik said Abu Talha said to Ummu Sulaim, that he heard the voice of the Prophet coming as a guest and knew he was hungry. He then asked his wife if there was something to eat.

She replied: Yes, There is some barley.

She put bread on my hands then sent me to go and call the Prophet. I went and found him sitting in the mosque with some people. The Prophet asked me whether Abu Talha had sent me.

I said: Yes.

He said, "with food?"

I said:Yes.

He then said to the people that were seating with him, "Stand up and let us go" I went along with them until we reached Abu Talha's house. I informed Abu Talha what happened. Then Abu Talha said to Ummu Sulaim:

The Prophet has come but with people and we do not have enough food for all of them.

Umm Sulaim said: Allah and His Messenger know best.

So Abu Talha went and welcomed the Prophet (P.B.U.H.). The Prophet said, "Bring what you have O Umm Sulaim". Umm Sulaim then brought bread and stew prepared from ghee. He (P.B.U.H.) prayed for the food, then called a group of ten from the people he came with to eat from it, they ate to their fill. He then called another group of ten from them and they also ate till they were satisfied, he continued similarly until they all ate and were satisfied. These people were seventy to eighty men in number.[37]

In another version, Imam Ahmad relates that Yunus Ibn Muhammad relates that Anas Ibn Malik said that Umm Salim sent me to the Prophet (P.B.U.H.), inviting him for lunch. I went and told him and he said:

"I am coming together with the people with me".

I said: Yes.

He said to the people he was with, "Proceed with me".

I went back to Umm Sulaim surprised by the number of people coming with the Prophet and she asked:

What have you done O Anas? The Prophet entered Umm Sulaim's house and asked if there was ghee.

She said: Yes, there is some. And she brought him a leather bag containing ghee. He then opened the bag and said:

"In the name of Allah, O Allah glorify your blessings in it". The Prophet took a portion of the ghee and from it ate eighty-something men, and still some ghee was remaining.

He gave it back to Umm Sulaim and told her to feed her family and neighbours.[38]

Miracles and Blessings that occurred on the day of the Battle of the Trench

Imam Al-Bukhari relates that Jabir Ibn Abdallah said: We were digging on the day of the Battle of the Trench, when we encountered a big rock. The Prophet (P.B.U.H.) was told of it and said:

42

"I shall descend into the trench".

He stood up and he had tied a stone over his stomach; we had not eaten anything for three days. He took up a spade and struck the rock once and it became like sand. I then requested permission from the Prophet (P.B.U.H.) to go home. When I reached home, I said to my wife:

I saw in the Prophet a condition (starving) I could not just sit and watch, so, do you have some food?

She said: I have some barley and a young she-goat.

I slaughtered the she-goat and ground the barley and we then made stew from the meat. Then I went to the Prophet (P.B.U.H.).

In the meantime, the flour had been kneaded and the meat in the pot was nearly cooked. I said to the Prophet (P.B.U.H.):

O Messenger of Allah I have some food, will you please come with one or two men?

He asked, "How many should there be?" I told him.

He said, "Many would be good. Tell your wife not to take the pot off the fire nor the bread from the oven till I arrive." Then he said to the emigrants and the helpers, "Let us go." They all stood up and went.

I went to my wife and said: The Prophet (P.B.U.H.), the emigrants, the helpers and those with them are coming over. She said: Did he ask you (the amount of food we have cooked)?

I said: Yes. The Prophet (P.B.U.H.) said to his companions, "enter, but do not crowd in". He begun breaking up the bread and putting meat on it, he would then cover the pot and the oven, and approach his companions, handing over the food to them. He continued breaking up the bread and putting meat on it and serving it to his companions till all had eaten to their fill, and some was left over. Then he said to my wife, "Eat from it, and send the rest as a present to the people for hunger has afflicted them".

A table of food descends from heaven

Imam Ahmad relates that Samura Ibn Jundab said: As we were seated with the Prophet (P.B.U.H.), we were served with *Tharid* (a dish of sopped bread, meat and broth), the Prophet ate and so did the people. People continued coming, eating and leaving until it was almost *Dhuhur*, then a man asked him: Was there anyone bringing more food on the table?

He said: From the world, no but from heaven.

Blessing of the food in Abu Bakar's the house

Imam Al-Bukhari relates that both Abdul Rahman Ibn Abu Bak said that, the people of Al-Sufa'a were people who were in poverty and the

Prophet (P.B.U.H.) had once said:

"whoever has food for two, it's enough for three and whoever has food for four it's enough for five or six.".......... Abu Bakar had some visitors, (we started eating when it was time for supper) By Allah! every time we took a morsel, the food increased, the guests ate to their fill.

When we finished eating the quantity of food was more than it was when we started eating. Abu Bakar then said to his wife: What is happening?

She said: No, it is now three times more than it was initially. Abu Bakar ate a bit and carried the rest to the Prophet and the people of Al-Sufa'a and despite their enormous numbers, ate from it (until they were satisfied).

Goat's liver is enough to feed one hundred and thirty men

Imam Ahmad relates that Abdul Rahman Ibn Abu Bakar said: We were with the Prophet (P.B.U.H.) and our number was one hundred and thirty men, then the Prophet (P.B.U.H.) asked, "is there anyone of you with food?" Suddenly, a man with unkempt hair was passing with goats he was rearing.

The Prophet (P.B.U.H.) asked him whether he was selling.

He said: Yes he was.

He then bought a goat from him, it was prepared, he then ordered the roasting of the liver. I swear by Allah, all the one hundred and thirty men took a piece liver from the prophet (P.B.U.H.), ate and got satisfied. We carried what remained in two large bowls on the camel.

Blessing of food in the battle of Tabuk

Imam Ahmad relates that Abu Hurairah said: In the day of (battle of) Tabuk, the food reserves were exhausted, so people starved till they asked the Prophet (P.B.U.H) to permit them to slaughter their camels for food. He gave them permission to do so.

On this, Umar said to the Prophet: O Messenger of Allah, if that is done we would suffer from lack of transportation, why don't you ask everyone to bring whatever is remaining of their food stuffs then you pray to Allah to bestow His blessings on it. The Prophet (P.B.U.H.) agreed. He therefore asked everyone to bring what they had. He prayed for the food, then he asked them to bring their food bags. He filled each and every bag with food till there was no one left with out a bag full of food.

Then he (P.B.U.H.) said: "I bear witness that there is no deity but Allah, and I bear witness that I am a Prophet and a Messenger of Allah, and he who meets Allah bearing the two without doubt will enter paradise".

Blessing Jabir's dates and paying debts of his father

Imam Al-Bukhari relates that Jabir's father died with debts.

He went to The Prophet (P.B.U.H.) and told him that his father left debts: I own nothing only the date tree, the harvest is not enough, so the Prophet (P.B.U.H.) went with him to the dates garden. He went behind one of the date palm and prayed for the blessing, then he ordered him to bring down the dates, I paid all the debts and the dates remained the same quantity as they were.

49

Blessing on Salman

Imam Ahmad relates that Salman said: When I said O Messenger of Allah how can such a small quantity of gold pay the big debts that I owe? He took them and kissed them, then ordered me to go settle my debts, which I did and there was still some left.

Blessing Abu Huraira and his dates

Imam Ahmad relates that Abu Huraira said, that he came once to the Prophet (P.B.U.H.) with a few dates and told him to ask Allah to bless them, the Prophet (P.B.U.H.) took them in his hands and prayed for them.

He then told me to place them in a container without scattering them out. I carried from it such and such (*wisq*) and gave out for charity. We continued eating from it and sharing it out for a very long time.

The Prophet's (P.B.U.H.) prayer when he had visitors and no food to offer them

Imam Al-Baihaqi relates that Waathilah Ibn Al-Asqa' said: The holy month of Ramadhan started while we were among the people of Al-Sufah. Whenever it was time to break the fast, each one of us would get an invitation from among the people.

A day came and none of us was invited so we woke up the next day fasting. The day after, the same thing happened. So, we all went to the Prophet's (P.B.U.H.) house and explained the situation. He (P.B.U.H.) sent a word to all his wives that if anyone of them had anything to eat, to send it over but in vain.

The Prophet then told them to gather around him, he prayed saying, "O Allah I ask you through your grace and mercy, for the two are in your hands, they are carried by none but you."

Suddenly, there was a knock on the door, when it was opened, they saw a roasted lamb. The Prophet ordered that, it be placed before us. We all ate until we were satisfied. Then he said to us, "We asked Allah through His grace and His mercy, this is His grace, as for His mercy, He has stored it for us".

Blessing of food in the house of Umar

Imam Ahmad relates that Dukin Ibn Sa'eed said: We were four hundred and forty when we went to the Prophet (P.B.U.H.) asking for food. The Prophet then said to Umar, "Stand and go fed them".

Umar said: O Messenger (P.B.U.H.) of Allah I do not have but what is enough for me and a baby for four months.

The Prophet (P.B.U.H.) said, "Stand and go feed them".

Umar said: O Messenger (P.B.U.H.) of Allah I have heard and will obey.

Umar stood and left and we followed him. He went with us to a room of his where he stores food, he opened the door and found it full with dates, all the people took what was enough for them, I was the last one to take; we left and the quantity of the dates was as when the door was opened.

The story of the poisoned goat meat

Imam Ahmad relates that Abi Rifai' the servant of the Prophet (P.B.U.H.) said: The Prophet (P.B.U.H.) was given goat meat as a present. I placed it in the pot and cooked it, the Prophet (P.B.U.H.) then entered and asked:

"What is this Abu Rifai'?"

I told him, it was goat meat given to us as a present.

He said, "Serve me the arm,"

I served him. He then said,

"Serve me another arm." I served him another arm. He asked again to serve him another arm.

I said to him : O Messenger of Allah a goat has only two arms.

The Prophet (P.B.U.H.) said: "If you could have been quiet you could have served me another arm and another until I stopped asking."

The Prophet (P.B.U.H.) liked to eat goats' arms, that is why the Jews in Khaibar poisoned the arm of a goat brought by Zainab the Jewish woman as present to the Prophet (P.B.U.H.). Then the poisoned arm told the Prophet (P.B.U.H.) about its poisoning.

Another version of Imam Al-Bukhari and Imam Muslim relates that, Anas Ibn Malik said: A Jewish woman gave the Prophet (P.B.U.H.)

54

poisoned goat meat. He ate from it then ordered that she should be brought to him. He asked her why she did so.

She said: I wanted to kill you.

The Prophet (P.B.U.H.) said, "Allah would never have empowered you over me".

They (companions) said: Should we kill her? He said no.

In the version of Abu Daud, Jabir Ibn Abdullah said: A Jewish woman from the people of Khaibar presented to the Prophet (P.B.U.H.) roasted, poisoned goat meat. The Prophet (P.B.U.H.) ate an arm from it and ate the rest of it with his companions, then he said to his companions, "Stop eating". He then sent for the Jewish woman.

He asked her, "Did you poison this goat?" The woman asked: Who informed you? He said, "I was informed by what I am holding in my hand (the goat's arm)".

She said: I said to myself if you are a Prophet, it will not harm you and if you are not a Prophet then your death will be a relief to us.

The Prophet (P.B.U.H.) forgave her. Nonetheless, some of the companions who ate it died. Imam Al-Baihaqi says that it is probable that she was sentenced to death after some companions died.

The tree moved towards the Prophet (P.B.U.H.)

I earlier mentioned a hadith narrated by Jabir Ibn Abdullah where two trees moved and covered the Prophet (P.B.U.H.). Here is another hadith reported by Imam Al-Baihaqi that narrated by Umar Ibn Al-Khattab that the Prophet (P.B.U.H.) was seated on top of the mount Al-Hajun distressed, grieved, disheartened and saddened by the insults and annoyance of the disbelievers.

He said, "O Allah show me a miracle today, I will not take hto anyone who falsifies me after it".

He then called a tree from a steep part of the city. The tree came towards the Prophet (P.B.U.H.) grooving the earth beneath. Then he ordered it to go its original position....The Prophet (P.B.U.H.) then said, "I will not pay heed to anyone who falsifies me among my people after this".

A tree stump cries because of the Prophet (P.B.U.H.)

Imam Al-Shafi' relates that Al-Tufail Ibn Ubay Ibn Ka'ab related from his father that the Prophet (P.B.U.H.) used to preach while leaning on a date stump. A man stood among his companions and asked the Prophet (P.B.U.H.) whether it was possible for them to make him a pulpit on which he would stand on and preach from during Friday prayers.

He said, "yes".

They then made him a three-stairs pulpit. Forth from, he stopped leaning against the date stump while preaching. As a result, the date stump cried in pity. The Prophet heard the cries, he went to it and comforted it by caressing it. It was later taken by Ubay Ibn Ka'ab (R.A.) when the mosque was renovated.

Imam Al-Buhari relates from Jabir Ibn Abdullah that the Messenger of Allah (P.B.U.H.) used to lean against a date tree during the Friday prayers. Then a person among the helpers said: O Messenger (P.B.U.H.) of Allah should we not make you a pulpit?

He said, "If you would like to". They made him one.

When it was Friday, the Prophet stood on

the pulpit and preached. Suddenly, the date tree cried a baby's cry. The Prophet (P.B.U.H.) descended the pulpit, hugged it and its cry gradually faded away. He said, "It cried because of the invocations of Allah that it used to hear".

Pebble's glorify Allah and greetings from a stone

Al-Baihaqi relates that Abu Dhar (R.A.) said: I can't mention Uthman except in good praise and that is because of something I saw. I was a kind of person who used to follow the Prophet (P.B.U.H.) around especially when he was alone.

That day I saw him seated alone, so I slowly went and sat beside him. Then Abu Bakar came, greeted him and sat on his right. Then Umar came, greeted then sat on Abu Bakar's right. Then Uthman came, greeted and sat on the right side of Umar. There were seven or nine pebbles in front of the Prophet (P.B.U.H.). He then took them in his hands and they started supplicated Allah, till I could hear, he then put them down and they went silent.

He took them again and placed them on Abu Bakar's hands, they glorified Allah until I could hear, he took them back. He then placed them on Umar's hands, they glorified Allah until I could hear, he then took them back. He then placed them on Uthman's hands, they glorified Allah until I could hear, he took them back and placed them down and they went silent again. Then the Prophet said: "Such is the Prophet's succession".

A stone greets the Prophet (P.B.U.H.)

Imam Ahmad relates that Jabir Ibn Samura said: The Messenger of Allah (P.B.U.H.) said: I know of a stone in Mecca that used to greet me before my Prophet hood.

Mountains and trees greet the Prophet (P.B.U.H.)

Imam Al-Tirmidhy relates that Ali Ibn Abi Twalib said: I was with the Prophet (P.B.U.H.) in Mecca, we were moving around; we did not pass a hill or tree except it greeted the Prophet (P.B.U.H.) saying: *Assalam Alaikum* O Messenger of Allah.

Earthly miracles consisting of Living Things

What involves animals, among the evidences of Prophet hood.

A camel prostrating to the Prophet (P.B.U.H.)

Imam Ahmad relates that Anas Ibn Malik (R.A.) said the *Ahlul Bait* among the Helpers had a camel that they used for irrigation, it refused to be mounted, so they went to the Prophet (P.B.U.H.) and complained. The Prophet (P.B.U.H.) told his companions:

61

"Stand up and let us go". They entered the farm and he went towards the camel, the helpers said:

O Messenger of Allah the camel behaves like a mad dog, it could harm you.

The Prophet (P.B.U.H.) said, "It can't harm me".

When the camel looked at the Messenger of Allah (P.B.U.H.), it came towards him and prostrated in front of him. The Prophet (P.B.U.H.) held it and led it to work.

The companions said: O Messenger of Allah this is just an animal, it has no brains and it has just prostrated in front of you. We have brains so we are more entitled to prostrating.

On this the Messenger of Allah said, "It is improper for a man to prostrate to another and if it were to be, I would have ordered a woman (wife) to prostrate to her husband due to the magnitude of his rights upon her. "

A camel complains of mistreatment by its owner.

Imam Ahmad relates that Abdullah Ibn Ja'afar (R.A.) said: One day the Prophet (P.B.U.H.) asked me to follow him. Whenever he wanted to relieve himself, he preferred either a hilly area or a garden of date palms. One day, he entered a shelter among the shelters of the Helpers, then all of a sudden, a camel came towards him, made a rumbling voice and shed tears. When the Prophet (P.B.U.H.) saw this, he caressed the back of its head and comforted it. In turn, it stopped crying.

He then said, "Who is its owner?"

A young man from the Helpers said: It is mine O Messenger of Allah.

Then the Prophet (P.B.U.H.) said, "Do you not fear Allah as pertains to this animal that He has placed under your ownership?" It complained that you neglect feeding it and mistreat it.

A camel tells the Prophet (P.B.U.H.) that the owner wants to slaughter it

Imam Ahmad relates that Ali Ibn Siyaabah (R.A.) said: I was travelling with the Prophet (P.B.U.H.) and he wanted to answer the call of nature; he ordered two small date palm to cover him, thereafter, he ordered them to go back to their original positions. Then a camel came towards the Prophet (P.B.U.H.), and put its neck to the earth then made a rumbling sound.

The Prophet (P.B.U.H.) said, "Do you know what the camel says? It claims that the owner wants to slaughter it". Then he sent for its owner. He (P.B.U.H.) said to him, "Will you grant it to me as a present?"

He said: There is nothing in my ownership more preferable to me than it. He (P.B.U.H.) then said to him, "I advice you to be kind and cautious"....

A wolf testifies to the Prophet's (P.B.U.H.) message

Imam Ahmad relates that Abu Saeed Al-Khudhiri (R.A.) said: A wolf hunted down a goat, the shepherd struggled with it and saved the goat. The wolf then sat down on its tail and said to him:

Do you not fear Allah? Do you deprive me of a subsistence that Allah has granted me?!!

The shepherd then said: How astonishing! A wolf talks to me like a human being.

The wolf responded: Should I tell you of something more astonishing? Muhammad (P.B.U.H.) in *Yathrib* (Medina) is informing people of events (stories) that occurred long time ago.

Then the shepherd came to Medina and approached the Prophet and informed him about his encounter. Then the Prophet called the people and told the shepherd to tell them his story.

The Prophet then said, "By He in whose hand my soul lies, The shepherd has spoken the truth. The Day of Judgment will never come until animals speak to human beings and a mans' limbs talk to him, and his thighs inform him of the deeds of his family in his absence".

The lion which accompanied Safina (R.A.) the servant of the Prophet (P.B.U.H.)

Abdul Razzaq relates that Safina (R.A.), a servant of the Prophet (P.B.U.H.), was left behind by the army (Muslim) in the land of the Romans.

As he was trying to catch up with them, he suddenly came across a lion. He said to it: O Abu Harith[58] I am a servant of the Prophet (P.B.U.H.), then proceeded to explain his situation to it. The lion then accompanied him till he reached the army.

A bird that complained to the Prophet (P.B.U.H.)

Abu Daud relates that Abdullah Ibn Mas'ood (R.A.) said: We were traveling with the Prophet (P.B.U.H.), then a man took an egg from a bird's nest. The bird came flapping its wings at the Prophet (P.B.U.H.) and his companions. The Prophet (P.B.U.H.) then said, "Who among you made this bird miserable?" Then a man among the companions said: I took its egg.... The Prophet (P.B.U.H.) said, "Put it back, put it back, as a sign of compassion to it."

أَلَمْ تَرَ أَنَّ ٱللَّهَ يُسَبِّحُ لَهُ مَن فِي ٱلسَّمَٰوَٰتِ وَٱلْأَرْضِ وَٱلطَّيْرُ صَٰٓفَّٰتٍ كُلٌّ قَدْ عَلِمَ صَلَاتَهُۥ وَتَسْبِيحَهُۥ وَٱللَّهُ عَلِيمٌۢ بِمَا يَفْعَلُونَ ﴿٤١﴾

Miraculous works of the companions

A walking stick that gleamed the path for its owner

Imam Al-Bukhari relates that AnasIbn Malik (R.A.) said: Two men from the companions of the Prophet (P.B.U.H.) went out of the Prophet's (P.B.U.H.) house on a dark night, they had what resembled two lamps in front of them (When they separated, it appeared that each one of them had a shining walking stick until they reached their people).[61]

In another version, Imam Al-Baihaqi relates that Abu Usaid Al-Ansari (R.A.) and another man among the Helpers were at the Prophet's (P.B.U.H.) house, discussing a matter till late in the night. When they went out of the Prophet's (P.B.U.H.) house, it was very dark. Each of them had a walking stick. When they started walking one of the two walking sticks gleamed like a torch and by that they saw where they were going. Then when they went in separate ways, each stick gleamed like a torch and they walked in light till they reached their houses.[62]

Story of the conversion of Al-Tufail Ibn Amru

Ibn Ishaq relates that Al-Tufail Ibn Amru (R.A.) was obeyed and respected in the clan of Dus. When he came to Mecca, the nobles of Quraish had a meeting with him wherein, they warned him of the Prophet (P.B.U.H.) by telling him that he should not listen nor speak to him.

He said: I swear they kept insisting until I made up my mind not to listen nor speak to the Prophet (P.B.U.H.). That day I went to the mosque and found the Prophet (P.B.U.H.) standing in prayer in front of the Ka'aba. I heard him reciting exquisite words (Qur'an).

He said: Then I said to myself; By Allah I am a person who is intelligent, a poet, I distinguish what is good from bad. It is upon me to listen to this person. If what he says is good, I will accept and if not I leave it.

He said: I kept waiting till he finished and went to his house. I followed him there and I said to him: O Muhammad, your people have told me such and such but I realized that there is something they are not telling me then, when I decided to hear you, I heard exquisite words. So, explain to me what you have come with.

He said: The Prophet (P.B.U.H.) then explained to me what Islam was and he recited the Qur'an to me. By Allah, I have not heard words more superior nor statements more just.

He said: I became a Muslim and I bore witness to the Truth and said, "O Prophet of Allah. I am a man who is obeyed by my people so, I will go back to them and call them to Islam. O Prophet, Ask Allah to grant me a miracle that will help me to do so".

The Prophet said, "O Allah grant him a miracle".

He said: So I went back to my people. When I was almost there, a light glowed like a torch between my eyes. I then said, O Allah not on my face I fear they might think that it is a curse. The light then appeared on my head. As I approached my people, they all gathered around me and my father came to me and I told him that I am a Muslim and that I am a follower of Muhammad (P.B.U.H.).

My father said: O my son your religion is mine.

I said to him: Go wash your body and clothes and then I will teach you what I was taught. My father then became a Muslim. My wife and my whole family became Muslims. My people refused to accept Islam, so I went back to the Prophet and he said, "O Allah guide the people of Dus, go back to them and call them to Islam. Be gentle and courteous with them."...

Resurrection of a donkey

Ibn Abi Dunia narrates in his book, "*Man a'asha ba'adal maut*" that Shaabi said that, a group of people came from Yemen from Jihad. One of their donkeys got tired so they forced it to move but it was not able to, it then fell down and died.

He stood and made ablution and prayed then said:

Allah, I came from *Dafina* fighting in your name, I worship you and I bear witness that you resurrect the dead.

I am asking you to resurrect my donkey. He stood beside the donkey and it rose and started moving.

$$وَٱلْخَيْلَ وَٱلْبِغَالَ وَٱلْحَمِيرَ لِتَرْكَبُوهَا وَزِينَةً وَيَخْلُقُ مَا لَا تَعْلَمُونَ ۞$$

72

Miracles that occurred when Halima Al-Saadia was breast-feeding the Prophet (P.B.U.H.)

Ibn Ishaq relates that Halima Bint Al-Harithy said: I went tc Mecca with a group of women from the tribe of Sa'ad, in search of children to breastfeed in a year of stiff starvation. We could not sleep at night because of the loud voices of babies crying for milk and I did not have milk to feed them. No one would accept the Prophet (P.B.U.H.), because he was an orphan.

They would say: We expect good (something in return) from the father. By Allah all the women I came with managed to get a child to breastfeed except me and there was none left but him (Prophet). I said to my husband Al-Harithy Ibn Ishaq: I swear I hate to go back with my friends without a baby to breastfeed so we went and took the orphan (Prophet). Al-Harithy said: Take him. You never know what blessing Allah might bestow upon us because of him.

73

After we reached home, I noticed that my breasts were full of milk. I breastfed the infant together with his brother, until they were satisfied. When my husband went to milk the animals, he found them with plenty of milk. What a blessed night it was. Allah blessed us in so my ways ever since we took the orphan.

Two years later, the two boys had grown. We took him back, the orphan's mother asked me to stay with him one extra year. After two or three months so had passed, the orphan and his brother (through breast feeding), were playing behind the house. His brother came to me horrified and said: I saw two men with white clothes opening the chest of my Qurashi child. We were perturbed by what happened, we returned the child to his mother.

When we narrated the story to the child's' mother, she told us that when she was pregnant, she dreamt that she gave birth to a bright shining light that by it, the castles of *Sham* (Syria and

Jordan) shone too. When she gave birth him, while in her hands, he raised his head to the skies, something ordinary babies cannot do...

Raising a young man from death

Ibn Abu Dunia relates that Anas Ibn Malik (R.A.) said: A young man from the tribe of Al-Ansar died; we closed his eyes and covered him with a clothe. A man among us suggested that we should inform the mother about his death. We agreed upon the suggestion.

When the mother came, she raised her hands towards the sky and said: O Allah ! I believe in you, I migrated to (Medina) your Prophet (P.B.U.H.), whenever I have difficulties I always turn to you and you sort them out, so I ask you O Allah do not let such a calamity befall me today. He said: The boy removed the clothe from his face and stood up.

The story of Zaid Ibn Kharija talking after death

Imam Al-Baihaqi relates that Sa'eed Ibn Musaib (R.A.) said that Zaid Ibn Kharija Al-Ansari died during the caliphate of Uthman Ibn Affan; they heard a voice from his chest, he spoke to them

Prophet (P.B.U.H.) heals the sick

Healing a boy with epilepsy

Imam Ahmad relates that Ibn Abbas (R.A.) said: A woman came to the Prophet (P.B.U.H.) with her son and said: This son of mine has madness, it attacks him during the day and night. The Prophet (P.B.U.H.) gently put his hand on the boy's chest and prayed for him. The boy choked and something black came out of his mouth.

A woman among the people of paradise

Imam Ahmad relates that A'taa Ibn Abi Rabaa said that Ibn Abbas said to him: Should I show you a woman among the people of paradise?

I said yes.

He said: This dark (complexion) woman came to the Prophet (P.B.U.H.) and told him: I have epilepsy and when it attacks me, I uncover myself so pray for me. The Prophet (P.B.U.H.) told her:

"You either have patience and have Paradise or I pray for you and your illness will be cured".

The woman said: I will be patient, but pray for me not to uncover myself . The Prophet prayed for her. Reported by Al-Bukhari and Muslim.

The Holy Prophet's (P.B.U.H.) prayer for the people of Madinah

Imam Al-Bukhari and Imam Muslim relate that Aisha (R.A.) said: When the Prophet (P.B.U.H.) came to Medina, Abu Bakar and Bilal fell ill.

She said: I visited both of them. Whenever their fever rose, they would recite poetry in praise of Mecca. I went back to the Prophet (P.B.U.H.) and informed him about my visit.

He prayed and said: "O Allah make us love Medina as we love Mecca or more, bless for us its food and shift its fever to Al-Juhfah".

The Prophet's (P.B.U.H.) prayer for a blind m

Imam Ahmad relates that Uthman Ibn Hunaifa (R.A.) said: A blind man came to the Prophet (P.B.U.H.) and asked for healing. The Prophet said to him, "You can either be patient

78

over your condition which is better for you, or I pray for you".

He then said: No. Pray for me.

The Prophet (P.B.U.H.) told him to take ablution and pray two *raka'ats* and recite this dua: O Allah I am asking you and I address you through your Prophet Muhammad, the Prophet of mercy, heal me. He repeated this dua many times till he had his sight restored.

The Prophet (P.B.U.H.) restores the eye of Qatada Ibn Al-Nu'maan on the day of Badr

Imam Al-Baihaqi relates that Qatada Ibn Nu'maan (R.A.) injured his eye during the day of Badr. The eye fell out from its socket, the companions then wanted to cut it, so they asked the Prophet (P.B.U.H.) and he said No. The Prophet took the eye, placed it back into its

79

socket and prayed. It healed and they could not differentiate between the eye that had been injured from the other.

The Prophet (P.B.U.H.) heals the broken leg of Abdullah Ibn Attiq

Imam Al-Bukhari relates that Al-Baraa Ibn Azib (R.A.) said: The Prophet (P.B.U.H.) sent men from among the Helpers under the leadership of Abdullah Ibn Attiq to Abu Rafa'a Al-Yahudy (a Jew) who used to insult the Prophet (P.B.U.H.).

When they arrived in *Jizan*, Abu Rafa'a was in his fortress. Abdullah managed to go into the fortress and kill him despite the fact that the fortress was in total darkness.

As he was coming out, he fell down and broke his leg. They then went back to the Prophet (P.B.U.H.). Abdallah said: The Prophet (P.B.U.H.) told me to stretch my leg, then wiped it with his hand and it healed.

The healing of Ali's eye

Imam Al-Baihaqi relates that Buraidah
(R.A.) said: The Prophet (P.B.U.H.) suffered from
a headache, so he never came out to the army
(battle of Khaibar). Thus, Abu Bakar took the
Prophet's banner and fought hard, he then
returned. Then Umar took the banner and fought
even harder, when he returned to the camp, the
Prophet (P.B.U.H.) said: "Tomorrow, I will give
the banner to a man who loves Allah and the
Prophet (P.B.U.H.). Everybody wished to be that
person.

In the morning, the Prophet asked for Ali
(R.A), he was told that he was complaining of a
sick eye. The Prophet sent for him, when he
came, he healed his eye and gave him the banner.
The Muslim army then fought under Ali's
command and won the battle of *Khaibar.*

His (P.B.U.H.) prayer for Abu Huraira to memorize knowledge

Imam Al-Bukhari and Imam Muslim relate that Abu Huraira (R.A.) said: They (people) say Abu Hurairah narrates a lot of (hadith) from the Prophet (P.B.U.H.), why don't the Helpers and the Immigrants narrate like him, as if they doubted me, I will tell you why it is so. The Helpers used to work in their farms and the Immigrants in the market. I always accompanied the Prophet, I was present when they were absent, I memorized when they forgot.

The Prophet (P.B.U.H.) said one day: "Who among you will grant me his cloth so that I empty my words on it, then he holds it to his chest and he will never ever forget what he hears?".

I granted him my outer garment and he emptied his words on it, then I held it to my chest, from that day onwards I never forgot anything he said.

82

Surely if it is not for these two verses, I would not have narrated a word to you,

"Verily, those who conceal the clear proofs, evidences and the guidance, which we have sent down, after we have made it clear for the people in the Book, they are the ones cursed by Allah and cursed by the cursers."

Prophet's (P.B.U.H.) Prayer for Saad Ibn Waqqas

Imam Al-Tirmithi relates that Sa'd (R.A.) said: The Prophet said : "O Allah answer Sa'd's prayer (dua') if he prays".

In another version Imam Al-Twabarani reports that the Prophet (P.B.U.H.) said: "O Allah answer Sa'd's prayer (dua')".

إِنَّ ٱلَّذِينَ يَكْتُمُونَ مَآ أَنزَلْنَا مِنَ ٱلْبَيِّنَٰتِ وَٱلْهُدَىٰ مِنۢ بَعْدِ مَا بَيَّنَّٰهُ لِلنَّاسِ فِى ٱلْكِتَٰبِ أُوْلَٰٓئِكَ يَلْعَنُهُمُ ٱللَّهُ وَيَلْعَنُهُمُ ٱللَّٰعِنُونَ ﴿١٠٩﴾

The Prophet's Prayer (P.B.U.H.) for Abi Talha's horse

Imam Al-Baihaqi relates that Anas ibn Malik (R.A.) said: People were alarmed when the Prophet (P.B.U.H.) mounted Abu Talha's, it was horse a very weak and slow. The Prophet (P.B.U.H.) started riding it, but it could hardly move. The companions rode slowly behind it. The Prophet (P.B.U.H.) then prayed for it and from that day onwards, it was never preceded by any other

The Prophet's Prayer (P.B.U.H.) for Juail Al-Ashja'i and his horse

Imam Al-Baihaqi relates that Juail Al-Ashja'i (R.A.) said: I participated in many battles with the Prophet (P.B.U.H.). I had a horse that was weak and slow and I was normally among the last soldiers. The Prophet (P.B.U.H.) retreated to where I was and said, "Move O horseman"

I said: O Messenger of Allah my horse is weak.
The Prophet (P.B.U.H.) whipped my horse and
said, "O Allah bless his horse for him". Thereon,
my horse became strong and fast, I had to hold on
tight due to the speed it gathered.

**Prophet's (P.B.U.H.) prayer for Abdullah Ibn
Abbas to have knowledge**

Imam Al-Bukhari and Imam Muslim relate
that, Ibn Abbas (R.A.) said: The Prophet
(P.B.U.H.) went to answer the call of nature, so, I
brought him water for ablution. When he came,
he asked, "Who brought this?"

They said: Ibn Abbas.

He said, "O Allah grant him a broad
understanding of the religion and teach him
ta'weel (exegesis)".

يُؤْتِى ٱلْحِكْمَةَ مَن يَشَآءُ وَمَن يُؤْتَ ٱلْحِكْمَةَ فَقَدْ أُوتِىَ خَيْرًا
كَثِيرًا وَمَا يَذَّكَّرُ إِلَّا أُوْلُواْ ٱلْأَلْبَٰبِ ﴿٢٦٩﴾

85

His (P.B.U.H.) prayer for Anas Ibn Malik to be blessed with wealth and children

It has been affirmed in Sahih Al-Bukhari and Sahih Muslim, that the Prophet (P.B.U.H.) prayed for Anas ibn Malik (R.A.) to be blessed with wealth and children. He was blessed with a garden that carried fruit twice in a year. It has also been affirmed in Sahih Muslim that he begot close to a hundred children.

In another version, the Prophet (P.B.U.H.) said, "May Allah prolong his age (he lived till the age of a hundred years)".

Prophet's (P.B.U.H.) prayer for Abu Talha Al-Ansari and his wife

The Prophet (P.B.U.H.) prayed for Umm Sulaim and Abu Talha upon the death of their son, that they be blessed (with children). They were blessed with nine sons and all of them memorized the Qur'an by heart.

The Prophet's (P.B.U.H.) prayer for Abu Hurairah's (R.A.) mother

It is affirmed in Sahih Muslim that Abu Hurairah (R.A.) asked the Prophet (P.B.U.H.) to pray for his mother, that Allah may guide her to Islam. Then he (P.B.U.H.) prayed for her.

When Abu Hurairah (R.A.) went back home, he found his mother taking a bath and after she had finished and came out of the bathroom, she declared: I bear witness that there is none worth to be worshipped except Allah and I bear witness that Muhammad is a messenger of Allah.

This made Abu Hurairah shed tears of joy. He then went and informed the Prophet (P.B.U.H.) and asked him to pray for both of them so that the faithful and righteous ones may love them... so the Prophet (P.B.U.H.) did so and the prayer was answered.

Abu Hurairah said: There is no believer except that they love us.

The Prophet's (P.B.U.H.) prayer for Saaib Ibn Yazid (R.A.)

It is affirmed in Sahih Al-Bukhari and others that the Prophet (P.B.U.H.) prayed for Saaib Ibn Yazid (R.A.) and wiped his hands over his (Saaib's) head. He lived long, until ninety four years of age still strong and healthy. His hair did not turn gray at the part of his head where the Prophet's (P.B.U.H.) hand passed over.

The Prophet's (P.B.U.H.) prayer for Abu Zaid Al-Ansari (R.A.)

Imam Ahmad relates that Zaid Al-Ansari (R.A.) said: The Prophet (P.B.U.H.) said to me, "Come close to me".... He said: He then passed his hands over my head and my beard and said, "O Allah make him handsome and preserve his good looks".

He said that he lived to over one hundred years of

age and his hair and beard was still black in colour.

He had no wrinkles on his face until his death.

The Prophet's (P.B.U.H.) prayer for AbdulRahman Ibn A'uf (R.A.)

It is affirmed in Sahih Al-Bukhari and Sahih Muslim that the Prophet (P.B.U.H.) prayed to Allah and asked Him to bless AbdulRahman Ibn A'uf (R.A.) when he saw him wearing a saffron gown on his wedding. Thus, Allah The Exalted answered the prayer and increased his wealth through trading and booty from battle. His wealth was abundant such that when he died, he left four wives and each one of them inherited four-eighth of eighty thousand.

مَّثَلُ ٱلَّذِينَ يُنفِقُونَ أَمْوَٰلَهُمْ فِى سَبِيلِ ٱللَّهِ كَمَثَلِ حَبَّةٍ أَنۢبَتَتۡ سَبۡعَ سَنَابِلَ فِى كُلِّ سُنۢبُلَةٖ مِّاْئَةُ حَبَّةٖ وَٱللَّهُ يُضَٰعِفُ لِمَن يَشَاءُ وَٱللَّهُ وَٰسِعٌ عَلِيمٌ ﴿٢٦١﴾

89

The Prophet's (P.B.U.H.) prayer for U'rwah Ibn Abu Al-Ja'ad Al-Maazini

Its affirmed from the hadith narrated by Shabib Ibn Gharqad, that he heard U'rwatu Ibn Abu Al-Ja'ad Al-Maazni saying that the Prophet (P.B.U.H.) sent him with one *dinar* to buy him a goat.

He bought two goats and sold one for a *dinar*, then went back to the Prophet (P.B.U.H.) and handed him a *dinar* and a goat. The Prophet (P.B.U.H.) asked Allah to bless him in his trade.

The Prophet's prayer against he who refused to eat with his right

Imam Muslim relates from Salamah Ibn Al-Akuu' that a man was eating with his left hand in the presence of the Prophet (P.B.U.H.).

The Prophet said: "Eat with your right!" (he ordered).

The man said: I am not able.

The Prophet then said: "You will not be able! Pride is what stops you". He said: The man was never able to use his hand again (paralyzed).

Prophet's (P.B.U.H.) prayer against seven idolaters

Imam Al-Bukhari and Imam Muslim relate that Ibn Mas'ud said the Prophet (P.B.U.H.) was praying in *Masjid Al-Haram* (Mecca) and Abu Jahal was seated with his colleagues.

They asked one another: Who is going to bring us a container with blood and the waste insides of a camel (after it has been slaughtered)?

One of them went and brought it, then they poured it on the Prophet (P.B.U.H.) while he was prostrating. At which they really laughed. The Prophet (P.B.U.H.) did not move from his position until Fatima (R.A.) came and removed what she could of it.

He rose and said, "O Allah I beseech you to punish the Quraish". The Quraish then complained, because they believed that a dua made in Mecca was answered directly. This made the Prophet rephrase and say, "O Lord I beseech you to punish Abu Jahal and I beseech you to punish U'tbah Ibn Rabia'h, Shu'bah Ibn Rabia'h, Walid Ibn U'tbah, Umaiyah Ibn Khalaf and U'qbah Ibn Abu Mu'eet". They were seven in number but Ibn Masu'd could only remember six.

He said: By He in whose hands my soul lies, I saw all the ones the Prophet mentioned being thrown into the well of Al-Qulaib in Badr.

The Prophet (P.B.U.H.) informed that the earth rejects an apostate

Imam Ahmad relates that Anas ibn Malik (R.A.) said: There was a man amongst us from the clan of Al-Najar who used to be the Prophet's

(P.B.U.H.) writer. He then ceased to be a Muslim, and as a result he fled. As he was fleeing, he met with some Jews who recognized him and said: This is the man who used to write for Muhammad.

They later killed him and buried him. The earth did not accept him, so with time it ejected him, they reburied him and he was ejected again while his face had already started decomposing. They had no choice but to abandon him

يَوْمَئِذٍ يَوَدُّ ٱلَّذِينَ كَفَرُواْ وَعَصَوُاْ ٱلرَّسُولَ لَوْ تُسَوَّىٰ بِهِمُ ٱلْأَرْضُ وَلَا يَكْتُمُونَ ٱللَّهَ حَدِيثًا ﴿٤٢﴾

Questions that the Prophet (P.B.U.H.) was asked and to which he answered in conformity to what was revealed in the holy scriptures before him

Holy Prophet (P.B.U.H.) informed about the Soul, Dhul Qarnain and the Companions of the cave

Muhammad Ibn Ishaq relates that Ibn Abbas (R.A.) said: The Quraish sent Ibn Harith and U'qba Ibn Abu Mu'ti' to the Jewish Rabbis in Medina to inquire about the authenticity of Muhammad's prophethood because they knew more about Prophets than they did. The Jews told them to ask the Prophet (P.B.U.H.) three questions:

(1) Ask him, what happened to the young men who disappeared during the first centuries?

(2) Ask him, about the story of the man who

traveled east and west of the earth?

(3) Ask him about the Soul?

If he answered these questions, follow him for he is a true Prophet.

Then the two returned to Mecca and informed the Quraish of their findings. Henceforth, they went to the Prophet (P.B.U.H.) and asked him the questions. He (P.B.U.H.) told them that he will answer them the following day (forgetting to say Insha Allah), hoping for a revelation (wahi).

Fifteen days passed without any revelation. People said: Muhammad promised us tomorrow and it is now fifteen days, he has not said a word about what he was asked.

The Prophet was perturbed by the word going around Mecca. Finally, Jibril came and revealed to him *Suratul Kahf* (Chapter of the Cave), in which were verses that answered their first two questions. Allah the Exalted says:

"And they ask you (O Muhammad) about the Ruh (the Soul); Say: 'The Ruh (the Soul) is one of the things, the knowledge of which is only with my Lord. And of knowledge, you, (mankind) have been given only a little ".[87]

We have talked about this lengthily in the book of *tafseer* (Tafseer Ibn Kathir), anyone who wants more details can refer to it. Allah the Exalted also revealed:

"Do you think that the people of the Cave and the Inscription (the news or the names of the people of the Cave) were a wonder among Our Signs....And never say of anything, 'I shall do such and such thing tomorrow.' "

أَمْ حَسِبْتَ أَنَّ أَصْحَـٰبَ ٱلْكَهْفِ وَٱلرَّقِيمِ كَانُوا۟ مِنْ ءَايَـٰتِنَا عَجَبًا ﴿١﴾

96

Then, Allah also mentioned the story of Musa and Al-Khidhir then Dhul Qarnain. Allah the Exalted says:

"And they ask you about Dhul-Qarnain Say: 'I shall recite to you something of his story' "[89]

The Almighty in the above verse and the ones that follow, explained and told his story.

What the Quraish asked the Prophet (P.B.U.H.) are happenings that conform with the stories found in the Books of *Ahl Al-Kitab* (People of Book), such are among the little truth found in them. Nonetheless, what has been distorted and changed is unacceptable because the Lord has sent down Muhammad (P.B.U.H.) truthfully and revealed a book to him which expounds to the people the controversies in reports and judgements.

Answers of the Prophet (P.B.U.H.) to the questions of the Jewish rabbis concerning the Hereafter.

Imam Al-Bukhari relates that Abdullah Ibn Salaam came to Medina and went to the Prophet (P.B.U.H.) and said: I will ask you three questions to which only a Prophet can answer. He said:

(1) What is the first sign of the Day of Judgement?

(2) Which is the first food that the people of paradise will eat?

(3) What makes a child resemble his father? And what makes a child resemble his maternal uncles?

The Prophet (P.B.U.H.) said, "The first sign of the Day of Judgement is a fire that will force people to move from the east to the west and the first food in Paradise is whale's liver and

98

regarding similarity of the child, if the man ejaculates first, then the child will resemble his father and if the wife ejaculates first then the child will resemble her.

Abdallah said: I bear witness that you are a Messenger of Allah.

Abdallah then informed the Prophet that if the Jews knew about his conversion then they would speak ill of him to the Prophet (P.B.U.H.), as they were a perversive people. The Jews came to the Prophet (P.B.U.H.), and Abdallah went inside the house. The Prophet (P.B.U.H.) then asked them about Abdallah Ibn Salaam and they said:

Our scholar and a son of our scholar. Our rabbi and son of our rabbi.

Then the Prophet asked them, "What if Abdallah converted to Islam?"

They said: May Allah distance him from that.

At that instant, Abdallah came out to them and said: I bear witness that there is none worth to be worshipped but Allah and Muhammad is his Messenger.

They said: He is an evil one and son of an evil one.[90]

In another version, Imam Muslim narrated that Thubaan, a servant of the Messenger of Allah said: I was asleep in the Prophet's (P.B.U.H.) house, when a Jewish scholar came and said: Assalam alaika O Muhammad. I pushed him and he asked me: Why do you push me?

I asked him: Why do you not say, O Messenger of Allah?

The Jewish scholar replied saying: I call him by the name his people call him.

Then the Prophet (P.B.U.H.) answered and said:

"My name is Muhammad by which my people call me".

The Jew said: I have come to ask you questions.

The Prophet (P.B.U.H.) said: "Is it going to benefit you if I answer you?"

He replied and said: I will listen and put what you say into consideration.

The Prophet (P.B.U.H.) said: "Ask".

The Jew asked: Where people are going to be the day the earth will changed to another earth and sky?

The Prophet (P.B.U.H.) said: "The people will be in darkness before the bridge *(sirat)*".

He then asked: Who will be the first people to cross?

He (P.B.U.H.) said "The Emigrants*(Muhajireen)* who were poor".

The Jew then asked: What they wibe served on entering Paradise?

The Prophet (P.B.U.H.)said: "The outermost part of a Whale's liver".

The Jew asked: What meal would they be served with for the day.

He (P.B.U.H.) said: "A bull from Paradise, which they will eat from its sides".

The Jew asked: What will be their drink?

He (P.B.U.H.) said: "From a spring called *Salsabila*".

The Jew then said: You spoke the truth and I have come to ask you about something that is not known by any among the people on earth except a Prophet or one or two people.

The Prophet then asked him, "Is it going to benefit you if I answered you?"

He said: I hear with my ears, I have come to ask you about a child.

The Prophet (P.B.U.H.) said, "A man's sperm is white and a woman's sperm is yellow, if they meet and the man's sperm is faster then the woman's then the child will be a boy by Allah's will and if the woman's sperm is faster then the man's then the child will be a girl by Allah's will".

The Jew said: I do believe that you are a Prophet (P.B.U.H.), then he went.[91]

The Jews acknowledge the Prophet's (P.B.U.H.) message and misrepresentation of the Torah

Imam Abu Daud narrates that Abu Hurairah (R.A.) said: A Jewish man and woman committed adultery, they then said among themselves: Take us to this Prophet for he is a

103

Prophet sent with moderate laws. If he is to pass a judgement other than stoning, we will accept.

They came to the Prophet (P.B.U.H.) and found him seated in the mosque with his companions.

They said: O Abu Qaasim! What would you do to a man and a woman who committed adultery?

The Prophet (P.B.U.H.) remained silent for a while and said, "I swear by Allah, He who descended the Torah on Musa, do you not find in the Torah judgement of adulterers".

They said: Coal should be applied to their faces and they should be flogged then, carried by a donkey around the village while people mock at them.

The Prophet (P.B.U.H.) saw a silent young man and asked him the same question and insisted that he should answer. The man said: The judgment in the Torah is stoning.

The Prophet (P.B.U.H.) then asked, "Who is the first man to break Allah's Commandments?"

The man said: A person closely related to the king fornicated and the king did not stone him. Then someone else from a different family did the same and the king wanted to stone him. The people went to the king and demanded that they will not allow him to stone their man until his relative was stoned.

So they had to sit and agree on what to do. The Prophet (P.B.U.H.) said, "I judge by what is in the Torah". The Prophet (P.B.U.H.) ordered the stoning of both of them.

Glad tidings of the Prophet (P.B.U.H.) by previous Prophets

The Qur'an and the Sunnah report the glad tidings of the Prophet (P.B.U.H.) in the previous revelation. Allah the Exalted says:

"Those to Whom we gave the scripture

105

(Jews and Christians) recognize him (Muhammad (P.B.U.H.) or the Kaaba) as they recognize their sons. But verily, a party of them conceal the truth while they know it [i.e. the qualities of Muhammad (P.B.U.H.) which are written in the Taurat (Torah) and the Injeel (Gospel)]"

Allah the Exalted says,

"So if they dispute with you (Muhammad (P.B.U.H.)) say 'I have submitted myself to Allah (in Islam)and so have those who follow me.' And say to those who were given the scripture (Jews and Christians) and to those who are illiterates (Arab pagans): 'Do you (also) Submit yourselves to Allah (in Islam)?' If they do, they are rightly guided; but if they turn away your duty is only to convey the Message; and Allah is All-Seer of His slaves"

Allah the Exalted says:

"Say (O Muhammad): "What thing is most great in witness?" Say: "Allah (Most-Great!) is witness between me and you; this Qur'an has been revealed to me that I may therewith warn you and whosoever it may reach. Can you verily bear witness that besides Allah there are other alihah (gods)?" Say: "I bear no (such) witness!" Say: "But in truth He (Allah) is the only one ilah (God). And truly I am innocent of what you join in worship with Him"[94]

Allah the Exalted says,

"Those who follow the Messenger, the Prophet who can neither read nor write (i.e. Muhammad SAW) whom they find written in the Taurat (Torah) (Deut, xvii 15) and the Injeel (Gospel) (John xiv, 16) – he commands them for Al-Ma'ruf (i.e. Islamic

107

Monotheism and all that Islam has ordained); and forbids them from Al-Munkar (i.e. disbelief, polytheism of all kinds and all that Islam has forbidden); he allows them as lawful At-Tayyibat (i.e. all good and lawful as regards things, deeds, beliefs, persons, foods), he releases them from their heavy burdens (of Allah's Covenant with the children of Israel), and from the fetters (biddings) that were upon them. So those who believe in him (Muhammad), honor him, help him, and follow the light (the Qur'an) which has been sent down with him, it is they who will be successful."

"Say (O Muhammad): "O mankind! Verily, I am sent to you all as the Messenger of Allah – to whom belongs the dominion of the heaven and the earth. *La ilaha illa Huwa* (none has the right to be worshipped but He) It is He Who gives life and causes death. So believe in Allah and His Messenger (Muhammad (P.B.U.H.)), the Prophet who can neither read nor write (i.e. Muhammad (P.B.U.H.)), Who believes in Allah and His Words [(this Qur'an), the Taurat (Torah) and the Injeel (Gospel) and also Allah's Words "Be!" – and he was i.e. Isa (Jesus) son of Maryam (Mary), and follow him so that you may be guided]"

"Can they (Muslims), who rely on a clear proof (the Qur'an) from their Lord, and who are witness [Jibril (Gabriel)] from Him recites (follows) it (can they be equal with the disbelievers); and before it, came the Book of Musa (Moses), a guidance and a mercy, they believe therein, but thise of the sects (Jews, Christians and all other non-Muslim nations) that reject it (the Qur'an), the Fire will be their promised meeting-place. So be not in doubt about (i.e. those who denied Prophet Muhammad and also denied all that which he brought from Allah. Surely, they will enter Hell). Verily, it is truth from your Lord, but most of the mankind believe not.

Allah the Exalted says,

"That he or it (Muhammad (P.B.U.H.) or the Qur'an) may give warning to him who is living (a healthy minded – the believer), and that Word (charge) may be justified against the disbelievers (dead, as they reject the warnings)."

Allah the Exalted sent Muhammad (P.B.U.H.) to the Jews, Christians, Arabs and Non-Arabs and all those who will be informed or hear about him are responsible.

The Prophet (P.B.U.H.) said, " By the One in Whose hand my soul lies, whoever hears my message from this *Ummah*, be he a Jew or a Christian then dies without believing in it except he is going to be among the dwellers of the Hell-fire.

The glad tidings of the Prophet (P.B.U.H.) are found in the revelations (books) of the previous Prophets before him from the first to the last of them – Issa Ibn Maryam (Jesus), who informed Sons of Israel of the coming of the Prophet (P.B.U.H.).

Allah the Exalted says:

"And (remember) when Isa (Jesus) son of Mariyam (Mary) said: O Children of Israel! I am the messenger of Allah unto you, confirming to you the Taurat [(Torah) which came] before me, and giving glad tidings of a messenger to come after me, whose name shall be Ahmad. But when he (Ahmad i.e. Muhammad) came to them with clear proofs, they said: This is plain magic"

The glad tidings of Muhammad (P.B.U.H.) are present in the Qur'an and in Hadith, and the teaching spread East and West... and if Muhammad (P.B.U.H.) was not a prophet, it could have adversely affected all the previous Prophets as it would have appeared that they were not truthful.

Allah the Exalted says:

"And (remember) when Allah took the Covenant of the Prophets saying: "Take whatever I gave you from the Book and *Hikmah* (understanding of the Laws of Allah) and afterwards there will come to you a Messenger (Muhammad) confirming what is with you; you must, then believe in him and help him" Allah said, "Do you agree (to it) and will you take up My Covenant (which I conclude with you)?" They said: "We agree." He said: "Then bear witness, and I am with yamong the witnesses (for this). Then whoever turns away after this, they are the *Fasiqun* (rebellious: those who turn away from Allah's Obedience)."[101]

Ibn Abbas (R.A.) said: Allah never sent a Prophet without taking a covenant, he sent Muhammad and ordered him to take a covenant from his people.

(Reported by Al-Bukhari)

Glad tidings of the Prophet (P.B.U.H.) in the previous Books

There have been found glad tidings of the Prophet (P.B.U.H.) in the previous Books. They are so many but I am going to mention but a few from the books of our past and present scholars.

In the first chapter of the Torah, in the story of Prophet Ibrahim(Abraham), Allah reveals to him glad tidings of a Prophet to come. Ibrahim thought that these tidings were of his son Ishaq

113

(Isaac) but then Allah revealed to him the meaning of it, that his son Ishaq is going to have a great number of offspring.

As for his son Ismail (Ishmael), the Almighty has blessed, He will make him great and will increase the number of his offspring. From his offspring there is going to be one who is good in character, has a gleeful soul and is pleasant in speech and that is to be Muhammad (P.B.U.H.).

In the story of Ismail from the first chapter, Ismail is going to have his hand over all the nations and all the nations will be under him and his brothers will be found living in all parts of this world. This did not become true in any Ummah (nation) except Muhammad's (P.B.U.H.) Ummah.

In the fourth chapter, in the story of Musa (Moses), Allah reveals to Prophet Musa to tell the sons of Israel that: *I will send down a Prophet from their relatives similar to you (Musa) and I will place inspiration in his mouth and they will all listen to him.*

In the fifth chapter, Prophet Musa during his last days, addressed the sons of Israel, and that was thirty-nine years from the year of *Teeh*, he reminded them the days of Allah and what He promised them and His benevolence upon them. He thus told them that Allah will send a Prophet (P.B.U.H.) from their relatives, who will enjoin them to righteousness and forbid them from evil and whoever disobeys him, he will be a failure on earth and will be punished in the Hereafter.

In the Zabur the book revealed to Prophet Daud (David), the *Ummah* of Muhammad (P.B.U.H.)has been described as a people of *Jihad* (holy war) and worship. It then described the Prophet (P.B.U.H.) as being the last stone that completes the building of a dome.

This confirms to what Allah says:

"Muhammad (P.B.U.H.) is not the father of any of your men, but he is the Messenger of Allah and the last (end) of the prophets. And Allah is Ever All-Aware of everything."[103]

The Book of Zabur, further described the Prophet Muhammad (P.B.U.H.) as a Prophet whose word will spread from sea to sea, he will unveil harm from his *Ummah,* he will save the weak who have no helper, people will be praying for him all the time and Allah will be blessing him everyday. His name will be mentioned until the end of time. Such a description marches none but Muhammad (P.B.U.H.).

The scroll of Prophet Ilyas

Prophet Ilyas (Elias) went out on tour with a group of his companions, when he saw Arabs in the land of Al-Hijaz he said: Look at these

116

people, they are the ones who will own your great fortresses.

They asked him: O Prophet of Allah, what will they worship?

He said: They will glorify the Lord Almighty in worship over everything ever worshiped.

From the scrolls of Ezekiel

Allah says: My best servant, I will descend upon him inspiration and he will be just to the nations, I chose him myself and sent him to the nations with laws that are true.

From the Book of Prophecy

A Prophet among the Prophets passed by Medina, then the Jews from the clan of Quraidha and Al-Nadhir followed him. When he saw them, he cried, they asked him what makes you cry O Prophet of God? He said: Allah will send a Prophet who will destroy your houses and hold captive your people. He (Prophet) said: The Jews wanted to kill him so he run away from them.

The words of Prophet Ezekiel

Allah said: Before you were even born I made you holy and chose you to be a Prophet and sent you to all nations.

The scroll of Sha'ya

O old woman be happy with this child which Allah presents you with, for through his blessings, places will spread out for you, the doors to your houses will rise, kings of the world will come to you from your right side and your left with presents and gifts... and this son of yours will inherit all the nations and own all towns and regions. Do not be frightened or be sad for the enemy will never ever harm you.

All became true in the time of Muhammad (P.B.U.H.). The old woman is the city of Mecca and it became as described above. Some (Jews and Christians) wanted to match this descriptions to *Bait Al-Maqdis* in Jerusalem but the descriptions do not fit it in all ways.

The scroll of Aramia

A star rose from the south, bright like lightening, its rays tore apart mountains. The is Muhammad (P.B.U.H.) and the rays is his Massage.

In the Gospel

Prophet Issa (P.B.U.H.) said: I am leaning in the highest paradise and I will send to you Al-Farqalid, a spirit of truth that will teach you everything and he does not speak of his own accord.

The intended meaning of Al-Farqalid is Muhammad (P.B.U.H.). Prophet Issa (P.B.U.H.) is reported in the Qur'an to have said,

"And (an announcer) giving glad tidings of a

119

Messenger to come after me, whose name shall be Ahmad."[104]

Imam Al-Baihaqi relates that Al-Alyan Ibn Asim said: We were seated with the Prophet (P.B.U.H.) when a Jewish man came and said: O Messenger of Allah.

Then the Prophet (P.B.U.H.) asked him:

"Do you believe that I am the Messenger of Allah?"

He did not reply but kept on calling: O Messenger of Allah.

The Prophet (P.B.U.H.) asked him, "Do you read the Torah?"

He said: Yes.

He then asked him, "Do you read the Bible?"

He replied: Yes. By the Lord of Muhammad if

you want, I can read the *Furqan* (Qur'an).

The Prophet (P.B.U.H.) said, "I swear by Allah Who revealed the Torah and the Bible, have you found me mentioned in them.

He said: We find in them your description, but we thought you would be from us. When you appeared we knew that it is you, but then we thought you are not the one.

The prophet said, "Where from".

He said: We find it written that seventy thousand people from your followers will enter Paradise without being held to account, but your people are small in number.

Then the Prophet (P.B.U.H.) applauded saying, "*Takbir*" twice, then said: "By the one in whose hand Muhammad's soul lies, indeed I am he, my followers are surely more than seventy thousand and seventy and seventy".

His (P.B.U.H.) answering of questions before the questioner speaks out

Imam Ahmad narrates that Wabassah Al-Asady (R.A.) said: I came to the Prophet (P.B.U.H.) intending to ask him all the questions concerning righteousness and sin, while a group of Muslims were seated around him inquiring on religious issues. I made my way through them so as to get closer to the Prophet.

As they were complaining, I said: Let me get closer to him for he is the most loved person to me...

The Prophet (P.B.U.H.) said, "Leave Wabassah alone, come close to me O Wabassah", he repeated this two or three times. I went and sat very close to him.

He said, "O Wabassah, should I tell you or will you ask me?"

I said: No, you tell me.

He said, "You came to ask me on righteousness and sin".

I said: Yes.

He said, "O Wabassah ask your heart and ask your soul –thrice – righteousness is what is appeasing to your soul and sin is what is abrading to your soul and causes hesitation in your heart no matter what people say or think".

وَبَشِّرِ ٱلَّذِينَ ءَامَنُوا۟ وَعَمِلُوا۟ ٱلصَّٰلِحَٰتِ أَنَّ لَهُمْ جَنَّٰتٍ تَجْرِى مِن تَحْتِهَا ٱلْأَنْهَٰرُ كُلَّمَا رُزِقُوا۟ مِنْهَا مِن ثَمَرَةٍ رِّزْقًا قَالُوا۟ هَٰذَا ٱلَّذِى رُزِقْنَا مِن قَبْلُ وَأُتُوا۟ بِهِۦ مُتَشَٰبِهًا وَلَهُمْ فِيهَآ أَزْوَٰجٌ مُّطَهَّرَةٌ وَهُمْ فِيهَا خَٰلِدُونَ ﴿٢٥﴾

The Prophet (P.B.U.H.) informs on what will happen in the future

This is a very vast chapter and we cannot tackle everything that comes under it, but we will try and pinpoint some of its main topics – *Allahu Al-Musta'an.*

Firstly: What is mentioned in the Holy Qur'an

Allah said in Suratul Muzzamil which is among the first surahs that descended in Mecca:

"He knows that there will be some among you sick, others traveling through the land, seeking of Allah's Bounty, Yet others fighting in Allah's course. So recite as much othe Qur'an as may be easy (for you), and perform As-Salat (Iqamat-as-Salat) and give Zakat, and lend to Allah a goodly loan. And whatever good you send before you for yourselves (i.e. Nawafil non-obligatory acts of worship: prayers charity, fasting, Hajj and

124

'Umrah), you will certainly find it with Allah, better and greater in reward. And seek Forgiveness of Allah. Verily, Allah is Oft-Forgiving, Most-Merciful"

It is common knowledge that Jihad was not prescribed but in Medinah after *Hijra*. Allah said in Suratul Iqtaraba:

"Or say they: We are a great multitude, victorious? Their multitude will be put to flight, and they will show their backs."

This happened on the day of Badr. Allah the Exalted says:

"Perish the two hands of Abu Lahab (an uncle of the Prophet) and perish he!

His wealth and his children will not benefit him!

125

He will be burnt in a Fire of Blazing flames!

And his wife, too, who carries wood (thorns of Sa'dan which she used to put on the way of the Holy Prophet (P.B.U.H.) or use to slunder him).

In her neck is a twisted rope of Masad (palm fibre)".[109]

He (P.B.U.H.) informed that his uncle Abdull'zza Ibn Abdul Muttalib who was nicknamed Abu Lahab, will enter Hell Fire together with his wife. Allah destined both to die non-believers and this proves Muhammad's prophethood.

Allah says that:

"Say: If the mankind and the jinn were to come together to produce the like of this Qur'an, they could not produce the like thereof, even if they helped one another."

And also says in Suratul Baqara:

"And if you (Arab pagans, Jews, and Christians) are in doubt concerning that which We have sent down (i.e the Qur'an) to Our slave (Muhammad SAW), then produce a Surah (Chapter) of the like thereof and call your witnesses (supporters and helpers) besides Allah, If you are truthful. But if you do it not, and you can never do it, then fear the Fire (Hell) whose fuel is men and stones, prepared for the disbelievers".

He informs that if all the human beings and jinn sat together to come up with a book similar to the Qu'ran, they will not succeed due to its eloquence, rhetoric, sweetness and judgments conveying what is accepted and what is not accepted. They will not be able to do so.

Allah the Exalted says:

"Allah has promised those among you who believe and do righteous deeds, that He will certainly grant them succession to (the present rulers) in the land, as he granted it to those before them, and that He will grant them the authority to practice the religion which he has chosen for them (i.e. Islam). And He will surely give them in exchange a safe security after their fear (provided) they (believers) worship Me and do not associate anything (in worship with Me. But whoever disbelieves after this, they are the Fasiqun (rebellious, disobedient to Allah)".

This happened as it is said above. Allah established this religion, triumphed it over all others and spread it to all horizons.

Allah the exalted says:

"He it is Who has sent His Messenger
(Muhammad (P.B.U.H.)) with guidance and
the religion of truth (Islamic Monotheism) to
make it victorious over all (others) religions
even though the *Mushrikun* (polytheists,
pagans, idolaters and disbelievers in the
Oneness of Allah and his Messenger SAW),
hate (it)".

This is exactly what happened. This
religion became universal, it defeated and
superceded all others and spread to the east and
west of the earth. Its name rose to climax in the
time of the Sahabah and those who came after
them and all other countries humbled before it.

Allah the Exalted says:

"Allah has promised you abundant spoils
that you will capture, and He has hastened

129

for you this, and He has restrained the hands of men from you; that it may be a sign for the believers, and that He may guide you to the straight path.[114]

The promise came to be, as the Muslims conquered Khaibar and Mecca.

Allah the Exalted says:

"Indeed Allah shall fulfill the true vision, which He showed to his Messenger [i.e. the Prophet Muhammad saw a dream that he entered Mecca along with his companions, having their (head) hair shaved and cut short] in very truth. Certainly, you shall enter Al-Masjid Al-Haram if Allah wills, secure, (some) having your heads shaved, and (some) having your hair cut short, having no fear. He knows what you knew not and He granted besides that a near victory".

Allah the exalted says:

"And (remember) when Allah promised you (Muslims) one of the two parties (of the enemy i.e. either the army or the caravan) that it should be yours; you wish that the one not armed(the caravan) should be yours, but Allah willed to justify the truth of His Words and to cut of the routes of the disbelievers (i.e. in the battle of Badr)".

The promise occurred in Badr (Battle) when the Prophet (P.B.U.H.) came out of Medina so as to capture the caravan of the Quraish, they were informed of Muhammad's (P.B.U.H.) plan. They came with an army of a thousand soldiers to defend their caravan. The Prophet (P.B.U.H.) and his Companions stood firm, confronted them with an army that's only a third of theirs, Allah aided his Messenger with an army of Angles. The Muslim army killed seventy of the nonbeliever's and captured seventy.

Allah the Exalted says:

"And (remember) when Allah promised you (Muslims) one of the two parties (of the enemy i.e. either the army or the caravan) that it should be yours; you wish that the one not armed (the caravan) should be yours, but Allah willed to justify the truth of His Words and to cut of the routes of the disbelievers (i.e. in the battle of Badr)

Imam Al-Bukhari narrated that Ibn Abbass (R.A.) came to the Prophet (P.B.U.H.) and said: Give me a portion of the wealth that we got from the battle.

The Prophet (P.B.U.H.) said to him: "Take".

He took as much as he could carry.

Allah the Exalted says:

"O you who believe (in Allah's Oneness and

in His Messenger Muhammad (P.B.U.H.)
Verily! The *Mushrikun* (polytheists, pagans,
idolaters, disbelievers in the Oneness of
Allah and in the Message of Muhammad
(P.B.U.H.) are *Najasun* (impure). So let
them not come near *Al-Masjidal-Haram*
(Mecca) after this year; and if you fear
poverty, Allah will enrich you if He wills,
out of His Bounty. Surely, Allah is All-
Knowing All-Wise".

This is the way it happened, Allah enriched
them from His Bounty by allowing them to
benefit from the spoils of war and from taxes paid
by the disbelievers.

Allah the Exalted says:

"We will show them our signs in the
universe, and in their own selves, until it
becomes manifest to them that this (the
Qur'an) is the Truth. Is it not sufficient in

regard to your Lord that He is Witness over all things?'''

Secondly: What is men:ioned in The Prophetic Tradition (Hadith)

The story of the scroll

The Quraish agreed to enforce sanctions on Bani Hashim and Bani Al-Muttalib (who were allies of the Prophet). They agreed that they should not help them in any way, nor marry from them, nor trade with them until they give up the Prophet (P.B.U.H.) to them. This sanctions were enforced to all, the Muslims among them and non-Muslims too.

The Quraish hang the scroll in the Ka'bah. Allah imposed over it termites which fed on it except the parts that had Allah's name written on it. The Prophet told his uncle Abu Talib about it. Abu Talib then went to the Quraish and said: In deed my nephew has informed me that your scroll has been eaten away by the termites except the parts of it that have Allah's name on it, so go and check, if it is not as he says, then I will hand him over to you. They went and found it as the Prophet (P.B.U.H.) had said. This led to the lifting of all the sanctions.

Completion of the religion and establishment of Muslims on earth

Imam Al-Bukhari relates that Khabab Ibn Al-Art (R.A.) said: We complained to the Prophet (P.B.U.H.) while he was seated under the shade of the Ka'ba.

We said: Why do you not ask for Allah's help? Why do you not pray for us?

He said, "Among the previous nations, a hole

used to be dug for a man and he is placed in it then they take a saw and cut him into two from his head. Others used to use a sharpened iron comb and rake off a man's flesh from his bones, and that never shook his faith.

Allahwill indeed complete this religion to the point that a man will ride from Sana'a to Hadhramaut without fear of none but Allah and a wolf's attack on his animals, but you people are too hasty".

The dream about Al-Hijrah, Uhud and the conquest of Mecca

Imam Al-Bukhari and Imam Muslim relates that Abu Musa (R.A.) said that the Prophet (P.B.U.H.) said, "I saw in a dream that I am migrating from Mecca to a land of many date palms. I thought it was Al-Yamamah or Hajar (a town in Bahrain) not knowing that it is Yathrib

136

(Medina).... And I also saw in a dream that I was brandishing a sword, then its tip broke off, that is what befell the believers in the battle of Uhud. Then I brandished another sword and it became better than it was initially, and that was the conquest of Mecca and the assembly of the believers. I also saw *naqr* (the death of my companions) and Allah's blessings, and the *naqr* was the death of the believers in the Uhud, and Allah's blessings were the *thawab* (rewards) we got on the day of Badr.

He (P.B.U.H.) informed of the killing of Umayyah Ibn Khalf

Imam Al-Bukhari relates that Abdullah Ibn Masu'd (R.A.) said: Sa'ad Ibn Muadh came to Mecca to perform U'mrah (minor pilgrimage), and stayed as a guest at Umayyah Ibn Khalf's house. Umayyah used to trade between *Sham* (Syria and Jordan) and Mecca and he used to stop over at Medina and stay at Sa'ad's house. As Sa'ad made *tawaf* (circumambulating)

Abu Jahal asked: Who is this making *tawaf*?

Sa'ad said: It is me Sa'ad.

The two exchanged words and Umayyah warned Sa'ad not to raise his voice to Abu Al-Hakam (Abu Jahal) for he is a noblest among the people of the valley (Mecca).

Sa'ad then said: By Allah if you stop me from doing my *tawaf* I will cut your relations with *Sham*.

Umayyah kept on insisting that Sa'ad should not raise his voice.

This annoyed Sa'ad and he said: Leave me alone, for I heard the Prophet say that Abu Jahal is going to murder you. By Allah Muhammad does not lie in his speech. So Umayyah went back and informed his wife and she also said: By Allah Muhammad does not lie.

When the Quraish set out for Badr,

Umayyah did not want to go. Abu Jahal said to him, you are among the nobles of the valley come with us even if it is for two days. So he set out with them and Abu Jahal killed him on the way.[123]

He (P.B.U.H.) informed of the killing of Ubay Ibn Khalf

Urwatu Ibn Zubair (R.A.) said Ubay Ibn Khalf a brother of Bani Jamha had sworn when he was in Mecca, that he would kill the Prophet (P.B.U.H.). When the Prophet (P.B.U.H.) was informed about it, he said, "Nay, I am the one who will kill him Insha Allah.

When it was the day of Uhud, Ubay Ibn Khalf carried a piece of metal saying: If I meet Muhammad, I am going to kill him. Ubay then came close to the Prophet (P.B.U.H.) but Musa'b Ibn Umair was shielding the Prophet (P.B.U.H.) with his body and he was martyred. Then the

139

Prophet (P.B.U.H.) ceased an opportunity and stabbed him with a spear. He fell down to the ground from his horse and he did not bleed from his wound. His people came and helped him while he mooing like a bull.

They said to him: What worries you? It is just a scratch. He informed them of what the Prophet said, "I will kill Ubay"

Ubay then said: By He in whose hands my soul lies, if this was to befall my people, they would have all died.

He then died and went to Hell.

Imam Al-Bukhari and Imam Muslim relate that Abu Huraira (R.A.) said he heard the Prophet (P.B.U.H.) saying, "Allah really gets angry at the man who gets killed by a Messenger of Allah for His sake".

He (P.B.U.H.) informed of how people will fight on the day of Badr

Imam Muslim relates from Anas Ibn Malik (R.A.) that Umar Ibn Khattab (R.A.) said:

The Prophet (P.B.U.H.) said, "This is how so and so will fight tomorrow Insha Allah".

He (Anas) said that Umar said: By He who sent him with truth, they fought just as the Prophet had said.

He said: They were dumped one after the other into a well, then the Prophet (P.B.U.H.) went and stood by the well and said, "O So Son of So! and O So Son of So and So! Did you find what Allah and his Messenger promised to be true? As for me, I found what Allah promised me to be true".

Then Umar said: O Messenger of Allah how do you talk to bodies that have no soul?

The Prophet (P.B.U.H.) replied: "They hear what I say but they cannot reply".

141

He (P.B.U.H.) informed that a man in the Muslim army is among the people of Hell

Imam Al-Bukhari and Imam Muslim relate that Sahl Ibn Sa'ad As-Sa'idi (R.A.) said: The Messenger of Allah fought against the non-believers in one of the battles. When the Prophet (P.B.U.H.) retired to his camp and the non-believers too returned to their camp, there was a man among the companions who was very brave and had fought very bravely. The companions were praising this man among themselves and the Prophet (P.B.U.H.) heard them and said, "He is among the people of Hell". Then a man among the companions said that he is going to accompany him everywhere he goes.

He said: They went out with him, when he stopped he stopped too and if he moved fast he moved fast too, he (the brave man) was then injured severely, so when the pain was to much for him to bear, he killed himself.

142

The man then went back to the Prophet (P.B.U.H.) and said: I bear witness that you are a Messenger of Allah. The Prophet said, "What makes you say that?"

He said: The man you said before a while that he is among the people of Hell and people were surprised, I decided that I will accompany him. I did follow him until I saw him wounded severely; thereafter he killed himself.

The Prophet said, "Indeed a man can do the deeds of the people of Paradise in what appears to the people and he is among the people of Hell. And a man can do the deeds of the people of Hell in what appears to the people and is among the people of Paradise".

يَـٰٓأَيُّهَا ٱلَّذِينَ ءَامَنُواْ لَا تَأۡكُلُوٓاْ أَمۡوَٰلَكُم بَيۡنَكُم بِٱلۡبَـٰطِلِ إِلَّآ أَن تَكُونَ تِجَـٰرَةً عَن تَرَاضٍ مِّنكُمۡ وَلَا تَقۡتُلُوٓاْ أَنفُسَكُمۡ إِنَّ ٱللَّهَ كَانَ بِكُمۡ رَحِيمٗا ﴿٢٩﴾

He (P.B.U.H.) inform of the grave of Abu Raghal

Imam Abu Daud relates that Abdullah Ibn Amr (R.A.) said: I heard the Messenger of Allah (P.B.U.H.) saying when we were going to Taif and passed by a grave:

"This is the grave of Abu Raghal and he was Abu Thaqif and he was among the people of Thamud. He was stopped from entering Mecca so when he went out, he was befallen by the punishment that befell his people at this place and was buried. They buried him together with bars of gold. If you are to dig up his grave, you will find the gold".

The people dug up and took out the gold.

He (P.B.U.H.) informed of the fall of Khosrau and Caesar

Imam Al-Bukhari and Imam Muslim relate that Jabir Ibn Samura (R.A.) said:

The Prophet said,

"When Khosrau falls there will be no Khosrau after him, and when Caesar falls there will be no Caesar after him. By He in whose hands my soul lies we will distribute their treasures in the way of Allah.[127]

This truly came to be during the time of the three Caliphs Abu Bakar, Umar and Uthman (R.A.). The Muslims conquered the two empires and distributed in charity the wealth of Caesar king of Rome and Khosrau king of Persia. This was a glad tiding to the Muslims, the two empires will never rise again. Thanks to Allah.

وَعَدَكُمُ ٱللَّهُ مَغَانِمَ كَثِيرَةً تَأْخُذُونَهَا فَعَجَّلَ لَكُمْ هَٰذِهِۦ وَكَفَّ أَيْدِيَ ٱلنَّاسِ عَنكُمْ وَلِتَكُونَ ءَايَةً لِّلْمُؤْمِنِينَ وَيَهْدِيَكُمْ صِرَٰطًا مُّسْتَقِيمًا ﴿٢٠﴾

He (P.B.U.H.) informed about the general peace in the nation

Imam Al-Bukhari relates that A'di Ibn Haatim (R.A.) said that: While I was seated with the Prophet (P.B.U.H.), a man came complaining of poverty and another came complaining of road robbery, the Prophet (P.B.U.H.) said, "O A'di have you seen Al-Khirah?

I said: No I have not seen it.

The Prophet (P.B.U.H.) said: If you will live long you will see a woman from Al-Hudij traveling from Al-Khirah to the Ka'abah and do Tawaf while with no fear of none but Allah...

إِنَّ ٱللَّهَ ٱشۡتَرَىٰ مِنَ ٱلۡمُؤۡمِنِينَ أَنفُسَهُمۡ وَأَمۡوَٰلَهُم بِأَنَّ لَهُمُ ٱلۡجَنَّةَ يُقَٰتِلُونَ فِى سَبِيلِ ٱللَّهِ فَيَقۡتُلُونَ وَيُقۡتَلُونَ وَعۡدًا عَلَيۡهِ حَقًّا فِى ٱلتَّوۡرَىٰةِ وَٱلۡإِنجِيلِ وَٱلۡقُرۡءَانِ وَمَنۡ أَوۡفَىٰ بِعَهۡدِهِۦ مِنَ ٱللَّهِ فَٱسۡتَبۡشِرُواْ بِبَيۡعِكُمُ ٱلَّذِى بَايَعۡتُم بِهِۦ وَذَٰلِكَ هُوَ ٱلۡفَوۡزُ ٱلۡعَظِيمُ ﴿١١١﴾

146

He (P.B.U.H.) informed Thabit Ibn Qais that he is among the people of paradise

Imam Al-Bukhari relates that Anas Ibn Malik (R.A.) that the Prophet (P.B.U.H.) asked where Thabit was, as he had not seen him for a while since he saw him.

Then a man said: O Messenger of Allah I will inform you about him. He then went Thabit's house and found him seated facing down.

He him asked: What is your problem?

He replied: I used to raise my voice higher than the Prophet (P.B.U.H.), so my deeds are void and I am among the people of Hell-Fire. The went back to the Prophet (P.B.U.H.) and informed him about him.

The Prophet (P.B.U.H.) said: "Go say to him: You are not among the people of Hell but indeed you are among the people of Paradise".

Thabit Ibn Qais died a martyr in the battle of Al-Yamama.

He (P.B.U.H.) informed Abdullah Ibn Salam that he is among the people of paradise

It is affirmed from an authentic Hadith that Abdullah Ibn Salam (R.A.) received glad tidings that he will die a Muslim and he will be among the people of Paradise. This is something people used to talk about when he was alive and it actually happened as the Prophet (P.B.U.H.) said.

Glad tidings to ten companions and those who attended the covenant of Hudaibiya

It is affirmed from an authentic Hadith that ten companions of the Prophet (P.B.U.H.) are among the people of Paradise. It has also been affirmed that the Prophet (P.B.U.H.) said that all those who attended the covenant of Hudaibiya will not enter Hell. They were one thousand four hundred or five hundred in number.

Information about the unknown that will happen in future

It is affirmed from Sahih Al-Bukhari and Sahih Muslim that Hudhaifah Ibn Yaman (R.A.) said: The Prophet (P.B.U.H.) stood and talked about all that is going to happen till Judgement Day.

It is also affirmed in Sahih Muslim that Abu Yazid Amr Ibn Akhtab (R.A.) said: The Prophet (P.B.U.H.) informed us about what happened and about what was going to happen till the Day of Judgment. In another hadith: The Prophet (P.B.U.H.) informed us about what happened and about what will happen until the people of Paradise entered Paradise and the people of Hell entered Hell.

He (P.B.U.H.) informed about Umar Ibn Khattab

It is affirmed in Sahih Al-Bukhari and Sahih Muslim that Aisha (R.A.) said: The Prophet (P.B.U.H.) said: "In every people there were *Muhadithun* , if there is one among my people then it is Umar Ibn Khattab.

In his biography there are occasions that prove this, for example Nafi' the servant of Ibn Umar (R.A.) said: He heard Umar on the pulpit saying: O Sariyah Ibn Zaanim the mountain!

People did not understand what he meant until Sariyah Ibn Zaanim arrived in Medina and said to Umar: O the Governor of the believers, we had surrounded the enemy but days passed without the enemy either attacking or surrendering, we were on a descended part of the earth while the enemy was in a fortress which was

150

on a high surface of the earth. I then heard a voice say: O Sariyah Ibn Zaanin the mountain. So we climbed the mountain and in no time Allah granted us victory over them.

He (P.B.U.H.) informed about Ummu Waraqah bint Nawafel

Imam Abu Daud relates that Umm Waraqah Bint Nawafel (R.A.) said: When the Prophet (P.B.U.H.) went to fight in the battle of Badr, she said: I said to him: O Messenger of Allah permit me to join you in the battle so that I can nurse the injured, Perhaps Allah might bless me with martyrdom.

He (P.B.U.H.) said: "Stay in your house indeed Allah the Exalted will bless you with martyrdom".

She used to be called Al-Shahidah (the martyr), she lived till the time of Umar's

Caliphate. She was killed by her two servants, who were later caught and crucified (according to Islamic law). That was the first crucifixion in Medina.

He (P.B.U.H.) informed of the Six signs that will occur close to Judgement Day.

Imam Al-Bukhari relates that Auf Ibn Malik (R.A.) said: When we were in the battle of Tabuk the Prophet (P.B.U.H.) said: "The six signs will occur close to the Day of Judgment: Death, conquest of Bait-ul-Maqdis, plague, the increment of wealth, a *fitnah* that will enter each and every Arab house, a truce between you (Muslims) and the Romans and then later they will come (and fight) in groups of eighty and each group has twelve thousand men".

إِنَّ ٱلسَّاعَةَ لَأَتِيَةٌ لَّا رَيْبَ فِيهَا وَلَكِنَّ أَكْثَرَ ٱلنَّاسِ لَا يُؤْمِنُونَ ۝

He (P.B.U.H.) informed of the death of Abu Darda

Imam Al-Baihaqi relates that Abu Darda (R.A.) said: O Messenger of Allah I am informed that you said there will be people who will turn apostates after they were believers.

The Prophet said: "Yes and you are not among them".

He said: Abu Darda died before the killing of Uthman.

He (P.B.U.H.) informed about what will happen to Uthman

Imam Al-Bukhari and Imam Muslim relate that Abu Musa (R.A.) said: I performed ablution in my house, I then went out saying that I was going to spend my day with the Prophet (P.B.U.H.). I went to the mosque and asked about him and I was informed where he was. I followed

153

him behind and found him seated at the edge of the well of Aris, having uncovered his legs and placed them both in the well. I entered and greeted him and sat next to the door. Then Abu Bakar came and knocked the door, I asked who that was.

He said: Abu Bakar. I informed the Prophet (P.B.U.H.) that Abu Bakar was requesting permission to enter.

He (P.B.U.H.) said: "Allow him in and inform him that he will enter Paradise".

He said: He went and sat on the right hand side of Prophet (P.B.U.H.). Then Someone knocked the door and I asked who it was.

He said: Umar Ibn Khattab. I informed the Prophet (P.B.U.H.) that Umar was requesting permission to enter.

He (P.B.U.H.) said: "Allow him in and inform him that he will enter Paradise".

He said: He went and sat on the left hand side of the Prophet. Then someone knocked the door again and I asked who it was.

He said: Uthman Ibn Affan. I informed the Prophet (P.B.U.H.) that Uthman was requesting permission to enter.

He (P.B.U.H.) said: "Allow him in and inform him that he will enter Paradise and a calamity will befall him".

He said: He went and sat in front of the Prophet (P.B.U.H.).

The calamity that will befall him is that which befell him at the end of his caliphate that led to his assassination.

وَٱلَّذِينَ ءَامَنُواْ وَعَمِلُواْ ٱلصَّـٰلِحَـٰتِ أُوْلَـٰٓئِكَ أَصْحَـٰبُ ٱلْجَنَّةِ هُمْ فِيهَا خَـٰلِدُونَ ﴿٨٢﴾

He (P.B.U.H.) informed of the *Fitnah* that will occur in the last days of Uthman and In the Caliphate of Ali

It is affirmed in Sahih Al-Bukhari and Sahih Muslim that Usamah Ibn Zaid (R.A.) said: The Prophet (P.B.U.H.) was standing at a high place and said: "Do you see what I see? I see the places of *Fitnah* within your houses and the places are heavily populated.

He (P.B.U.H.) informed about the conflict between Aisha and Ali

Imam Ahmad relates from Aisha (R.A.) that: When she was passing by the well of Bani Amir (heading to the Battle of the Camel) dogs barked. She asked: Where is this? They told her, the waters of Al-Hawab.

She said: I am thinking of going back.

156

Some of the people she was with said: Nay rather continue so that the Muslims see you, Allah may reconcile between the two of you.

She said: The Prophet (P.B.U.H.) said to us one day: "How do the dogs of Al-Hawab (near Basra) bark at one of you?"

He (P.B.U.H.) informed about the killing of Talha and Zubair during the Caliphate of Ali

Imam Al-Tabarani narrated that Ibn Abbas (R.A.) said: When the companions of Ali arrived at Basra, the people were against Talha and Zabair. Ali said: I swear the people of Basra will kill Talha and Zubair and they will fight you from Kufah with an army of five thousand five hundred and fifty men. So when we reached Kufah I was anxious to see whether it truly will happen as he said or if it is just deception of the Arabs... then I met a man among the soldiers and I asked him, I swear he said what Ali said.

Ibn Abbas said: That is what the Messenger of Allah had informed.

It is affirmed in Sahih Al-Bukhari and Sahih Muslim that Abu Hurairah (R.A.) said: The Prophet (P.B.U.H.) said: "It shall not be the Day of Judgment until two great groups fight, and there will be a great loss of life's from both sides yet they are one people".

The two groups were the people who fought the battle of the Camel and *Seifein*, for they fought one another yet they were all Muslims.

He (P.B.U.H.) informed about the killing of Amar

Safwan Ibn Amr said: The people of Sham were sixty thousand, twenty thousand of them lost their lives. The people of Iraq were a hundred and twenty thousand, of whom forty thousand lost their lives. Ali and his people were closer to what was right and Mua'wiyah and his people had oppressed them. In Sahih Muslim Abu Qatada said, the Prophet (P.B.U.H.) said to Amar: "You will be attacked by an oppressive group and be killed".

He (P.B.U.H.) informed about Al-Khawaarij, their deard character

Imam Al-Bukhari relates that Abu Said Al-Khudhary (R.A.) said: We were with the Prophet (P.B.U.H.) when a man from the tribe of Tamim came and said: O Messenger of Allah be just.

The Prophet (P.B.U.H.) said: *Wailak !* If I am not just who will be?"

Umar said: O Messenger of Allah (P.B.U.H.), permit me to cut of his head.

۞ إِنَّ ٱللَّهَ يَأْمُرُ بِٱلْعَدْلِ وَٱلْإِحْسَـٰنِ وَإِيتَآيِ ذِى ٱلْقُرْبَىٰ وَيَنْهَىٰ عَنِ ٱلْفَحْشَآءِ وَٱلْمُنكَرِ وَٱلْبَغْيِ ۚ يَعِظُكُمْ لَعَلَّكُمْ تَذَكَّرُونَ ﴿٩٠﴾

159

He (P.B.U.H.)said: "Leave him. He will have companions whom, you will despise your prayers and fast to theirs, they will be reading Qur'an a lot, but Allah will not accept their acts of worship. They will leave the religion like an arrow, released from the bow. Their sign is, that there will be a man with a dark complexion among them who have something like a woman's breast between his shoulder and his hand. They will emerge when Muslims differentiate (what occurred between Mua'wiyah and Ali may Allah bless them both).

يُخَٰدِعُونَ ٱللَّهَ وَٱلَّذِينَ ءَامَنُوا۟ وَمَا يَخْدَعُونَ إِلَّآ أَنفُسَهُمْ وَمَا يَشْعُرُونَ ﴿١﴾

إِنَّ ٱلْمُنَٰفِقِينَ يُخَٰدِعُونَ ٱللَّهَ وَهُوَ خَٰدِعُهُمْ وَإِذَا قَامُوٓا۟ إِلَى ٱلصَّلَوٰةِ قَامُوا۟ كُسَالَىٰ يُرَآءُونَ ٱلنَّاسَ وَلَا يَذْكُرُونَ ٱللَّهَ إِلَّا قَلِيلًا ﴿١٤٢﴾

160

Summary

The emergence of Al-Khawarij has been narrated in many of hadith of the Prophet (P.B.U.H.), something that has made the scholars to agree on the authenticity of the narrations about it and that it occurred during Ali's Caliphate.

He (P.B.U.H.) informs about the killing of Ali and how it will happen

Another version of Imam Ahmad relates that Al-Fadhalah Al-Ansari (R.A.) said:......Ali said: The Prophet (P.B.U.H.) promised me that I will not die until I take authority (Caliph) then my beard is tinged with blood.

Ali was stubbed outside his door by a man known as Abdul Rahman Ibn Maljim who was a Khawarij (from among the deserters whom the Prophet (P.B.U.H.) prophesied of their emergence), when he was going for Fajr prayers. Ali lived two days after the stubbing before he died. Abdul Rahman Al-Maljim was caught and sentenced to death after Ali's death.

He (P.B.U.H.) informs about what Hassan will do after his father's death.

Imam Al-Bukhari relates that Abu Bakrah (R.A.) said: The Prophet (P.B.U.H.) came with Hassan and ascended with him on the pulpit and said: This son of mine is a *Sayeed* (master) and Allah will reconcile two groups of Muslims through him.

It occurred just as the Prophet (P.B.U.H.) had informed. Hassan Ibn Ali was made a Caliph in Basra after the death of his father, but for the sake of peace between the Muslims he sacrificed his post and stepped down for Mua'wiyah, thus the two fighting factions reconciled. Mua'wiyyah became the Caliph of the Islamic State. Thus, that year came to be known as The Year of Unity. The

Prophet bore witness that the two groups or factions that fought one another were both Muslim. This proves those who say otherwise wrong. This further proved the prophecy of Prophet Muhammad (P.B.U.H.) who does not speak of his own accord but rather from inspiration.

He (P.B.U.H.) informed about the battle on sea near Cyprus and the war with the Romans

Imam Al-Bukhari and Imam Muslim relate that Anas Ibn Malik (R.A.) said: The Prophet (P.B.U.H.) used to visit Umm Haraam Bint Mulhan, (the Prophet was her Mahram) who used to feed him and rid of lice from his hair. That day the Prophet (P.B.U.H.) visited her, she fed him and started ridding of lice from his hair, then he fell asleep. He (P.B.U.H.) woke up laughing.

She said: I asked him: What makes you laugh.

He (P.B.U.H.) said: "People from my Ummah fought in Jihad sailing in the sea of *Al-Muluk* (Mediterranean) victoriously".

She said: O the Messenger (P.B.U.H.) of Allah, pray to Allah that I be among them. He prayed for her then laid his head and slept. He (P.B.U.H.) woke up laughing again.

She asked him: What makes you laugh?

He said: A group of my people fought in Jihad.

She said: O the Messenger (P.B.U.H.) of Allah, pray to Allah that I be among them. He said: "you would be among the first ones".

It occurred during the time of Mua'wiyah Ibn Abu Sufyan, she and her husband Ubadah Ibn Swamit were among those who

164

fought together with Mua'wiyah in the sea. She later died from a horse fall after coming back from the sea.

Imam Al-Bukhari relates that Umm Haraam heard the Prophet say that: "The first army from my Ummah to fight on sea have been forgiven".

There are three evidences of Prophethood

1. Battle of the sea

It occurred during the Caliphate of Uthman Ibn Afan, in the year 27 Hijrah under the command of Mua'wiyah. Who was the governor of Sham.

2. Battle of Constantinople

It occurred during the Caliphate of Mua'wiyah Ibn Abu Sufyan in the year 52 Hijrah and together with Abu Ayub and Khalid Ibn Zaid who died there. Umm Haraam was not with them because she died before the battle. The tied evidence is His (P.B.U.H.) prophecy that a woman will among the first and not the last. It all happened as he said (P.B.U.H.).

3. He informed of the conquest of India.

Imam Ahmad relates that Abu Huraira (R.A.) said: The Prophet (P.B.U.H.) said to me: "My people will conquer Sind and India".

The Muslims fought in India during the time of Mua'wiyah in the year 44 Hijri… They fought king Al-Jahiil Mahmud Ibn Sabaktakin the owner of the highland, which is four hundred miles from the border with India. The Muslims fought and captured India and entered the land of Al-Somaniyat broke their idols, which they were worshipping and returned safely and victoriously.

The glad tidings for Abdallah Ibn Salam

Imam Muslim relates that Khurshah Ibn Al-Hur said: I was seated in the mosque of Medina with a group of students listening to a Sheikh. The Sheikh was Abdullah Ibn Salaam (R.A.). When Abdallah stood up, people said: Anyone who would like to see a man among the people of paradise should look at him. I swear... I followed him until we were almost going out of Medinah and entered his house. I requested permission to enter and he welcomed me.

He said: What do you need son of my brother?

I said: I heard people talking about you saying that you are among the people of Paradise... So I just want to be with you.

He said: Allah knows best about the people of Paradise, I will tell you about what they say. One day when I was asleep, a man came and told wake me up. Took me by his hands and we started walking suddenly we were at *Jawad* a road on the left, he asked me not to take that road as it was for the people of the left side. Then there was another road on my right hand side which was straight. He asked me to take the it, we approached a mountain and he said to me: Climb it. I tried but I kept sliding back, I tried again and again but in vain. We continued moving until we reached a post who's bottom is on earth and top in the sky.

He said: Climb...

I said: How do I do it while its top is the sky? He took me by his hands and left me clinching by the post. I remained clinching to till morning. When I woke up, I went to the Prophet (P.B.U.H.) and inform him about my dream.

He said: "The path on your left is for the people of the left-hand side and the path that was on your right is for the people of the right-hand side, the mountain is the place of the martyrs and you are not among them, the post is Islam and you will continue being one till you die".

Imam Al-Baihaqi said that Abdullah Ibn Salaam died in the year 43 AH, which is also mentioned by Abu Ubaid.

He (P.B.U.H.) informed about the death of Maimunah Bint Al-Harith at Sarif

Imam Al-Bukhari relates that Yazid Ibn Al-Aswam said: Maimunah (R.A.) fell sick in Mecca, where she had no relatives…She said: I will not die in Mecca…The Messenger of Allah (P.B.U.H.) informed that I will not die in Mecca. So they carried and brought her to Sarif (near Tane'em), at the same tree under which the Prophet (P.B.U.H.) married her. Thereafter she died. This was on the year 51 A.H.

إِنَّ ٱللَّهَ عِندَهُۥ عِلۡمُ ٱلسَّاعَةِ وَيُنَزِّلُ ٱلۡغَيۡثَ وَيَعۡلَمُ مَا فِى ٱلۡأَرۡحَامِ ۖ وَمَا تَدۡرِى نَفۡسٌ مَّاذَا تَكۡسِبُ غَدًا ۖ وَمَا تَدۡرِى نَفۡسٌۢ بِأَىِّ أَرۡضٍ تَمُوتُ ۚ إِنَّ ٱللَّهَ عَلِيمٌ خَبِيرُۢ ﴿٣٤﴾

After my death there will be selfishness and egoism

Imam Al-Bukhari relates that Ibn Mas'ud (R.A.) said that the Prophet (P.B.U.H.) said: "There will be selfishness and egoism after my death".

The people said: O Messenger (P.B.U.H.) what do you command us to do?

He said: "Execute the duties that are upon you and ask Allah for what is yours".

Imam Al-Bukhari also relates that Abu Hurairah (R.A.) said: I heard the Messenger (P.B.U.H.) say: "My *Ummah* will perish in the hands of youth from Quraish".

He said: The youth is Marwan!

Abu Hurairah said: if you want me to mention them: Bani *fulan* and Ban*fulan* (this clan and that clan).[150]

He (P.B.U.H.) informed about the killing of Hussein Ibn Ali

Imam Ahmad relates that Anas Ibn Malik (R.A.) said that the Angel of Rain asked to come to the Prophet (P.B.U.H.) and was allowed to do so.

The Prophet (P.B.U.H.) said to Umm Salamah: "Guard the door so that no one enters".

Then came Hussein Ibn Ali, he jumped until he managed to enter, he climbed on to the shoulders of the Prophet (P.B.U.H.).

The Angel asked the Prophet (P.B.U.H.): Do you love him.

The Prophet (P.B.U.H.) said: "Yes".

The angel said: Your *Ummah* will kill him and if you so wish, I will show you where he will be killed.

He said: The Angel clapped his hands and showed the Prophet red sand.

171

He said: Umm Salamah then took the sand and wrapped it in a piece of cloth.

He said: We used hear that he will be killed at Bakrballa

He (P.B.U.H.) informs about the killing of the Turks

Imam Al-Bukhari relates that Abu Huraira (R.A.) heard the Prophet (P.B.U.H.) say: "It shall not be Judgment Day until you fight people with hairy shoes, small eyes and round flat red faces, flat noses, and have no knowledge on Islam...

The Muslims fought the Turks in last era of the companions of the Prophets (P.B.U.H.). They fought Ilqan the Great who suffered a severe defeat.

He (P.B.U.H.) informed about false Prophets

It is affirmed in Sahih Al-Bukhari and Sahih Muslim that Jabir Ibn Samurah (R.A.) said: The Prophet (P.B.U.H.) said: "There will be thirty Liars, Imposters before the Day of judgement. All of them will claim to be prophets".

In another version:

Imam Al-Baihaqi, he relates that Abdallah Ibn Zubair (R.A.) said:

The Messenger of Allah said: "The day of judgment will not come until thirty Liars emerge, among them Musailamah, Al-Asnah, Al-Mukhtar and from evil tribes of the Arabs: Bani Umaiyyah, Bani Hanifah and Bani Thakif.

إِنَّ ٱلسَّاعَةَ لَآتِيَةٌ لَّا رَيْبَ فِيهَا وَلَٰكِنَّ أَكْثَرَ ٱلنَّاسِ لَا يُؤْمِنُونَ ﴿٥٩﴾

173

He (P.B.U.H.) informs the ending of his century after one hundred years

It is affirmed in Sahih Al-Bukhari and Sahih Muslim that Ibn Umar (R.A.) said: The Prophet (P.B.U.H.) led us in Isha prayers during his last days and after prayer he stood and said: "Have you all seen this night? Indeed after one hundred years there will be no one remaining on this earth".

Ibn Umar said: People misunderstood the words of the Prophet (P.B.U.H.) in this hadith concerning one hundred years. What the Prophet (P.B.U.H.) said was: "there will be no one remaining from the ones on earth today". Meaning that all of them would have passed away.

He (P.B.U.H.) informs about twelve imams – all of them from Quraish

The twelve imams are not the ones whom the Rafidha (Shi'a) claim they are. They only claim for Ali Ibn Abu Talib, his two sons (Hassan and Hussein) and Mahdi whom they wait for. Among the twelve imams mentioned in the hadith are; Abu Bakar, Umar, Uthman, Ali, and Umar Ibn AbdulAziz. It is affirmed in Sahih Al-Bukhari and Sahih Muslim that the Prophet (P.B.U.H.) said: "This authority will not cease to be until there are twelve caliphs, all of them from the Quraish".

Another version of Abu Daud relates that Jabir Ibn Samurah said: I heard the Messenger of Allah saying: The order will be firm until twelve Caliphs rule and all the people gather under them.

Sahih Al-Bukhari relates that Mua'wiyyah Ibn Abu Sufyan said: I heard the Prophet (P.B.U.H.)

saying: The twelve Caliphs are from the Quraish.

He (P.B.U.H.) gave signs of Malik Ibn Anas

Imam Al-Tirmidhy relates from the hadith of Ibn Uaina narrated by Abu Huraira (R.A.) that: Soon people will start hitting the backs of Camels (Travelling) to seek knowledge, then they will not find someone more knowledgeable than the scholar in Medina".

Imam Al-Tirmidhy said: That is Malik Ibn Anas. Abdulrazaq said that Malik died in the year of 179 A.H.

He (P.B.U.H.) gave signs of Muhammad Ibn Idris Al-Shafi'

Imam Abu Daud relates that Abdullah said: The Prophet (P.B.U.H.) said: "Do not insult Quraish, for indeed a scholar from them will fill the earth with knowledge... O Allah, you let difficulty befall the first ones so grant your favor upon the last ones.

Al-Hafidh Abu Naim Al-Asbahani said: That is Al-Shafi'.

Al-Shafi' died in the year 204 A.H.

He (P.B.U.H.) informed about a fire which will be seen in the land of Al-Hijaz

When this fire was burning in the land of Al-Hijaz its blazes shone on the neck of the camels in Basra, this occurred in the year 654 A.H.

Imam Al-Bukhari relates that Abu Huraira (R.A.) said that: The Prophet (P.B.U.H.) said: "The Day of Judgment will not come until a fire burns from the land of Al-Hijaz and by it the necks of the camels in Basra shine".

The Historians and other scholars have also

mentioned of its occurrence in year 654 A.H.

The Story of Al-Alaa Ibn Al-Hadhramy

Imam Al-Baihaqi relates that Anas Ibn Malik (R.A.) said that:...Umar Ibn Khattab prepared an army together with Al-Alaa Ibn Al-Hadhramy.

Anas said: I attended this battle so when we arrived at the battlefield, we found our opponents had already covered all the water sources. It was a very hot day, we became so thirsty and our animals too.

Al-Hadhramy led us in a two *raka'ats* prayer then raised his hands to the sky and not a single cloud could be seen. I swear that he before he descended his hands, Allah had already sent a strong wind carrying thick clouds. It poured down heavily. We thus collected water to drink, filled all our containers and quenched our thirst and that

178

of our animals too. We followed our enemy but they had already crossed the gulf to the island.

He stood at the gulf and said: O Most High O Most Powerful, O Most Kind O Most Generous,...Then said to us: Cross, by the name of Allah.

He said: We crossed the sea on our animals, the water hardly reached the hoofs of our animals. It was not long before we caught up with our enemies, we confronted them and Allah blessed us with a victory over them.

The hadith also mentioned the death of Al-Hadhramy, they buried him in a land that does not accept the dead. So they dug another grave in which they would transfer the body. When it was time to rebury they could not find his body, all they saw in the initial grave was a bright light. They covered the grave and left.

The Story of Abu Muslim Al-Khulani

Imam Al-Baihaqi relates that Sulaiman Ibn
Al-Mughirah said: Abu Muslim Al-Kulani
walked on water then turned his people and
asked: Has any one of you lost anything?

Muhammad Ibn Ziyad relates from Abu
Muslim that when they were fighting in the land
of the Romans, they sometimes come across a
river and he would say: Cross in the name of
Allah.

Ibn Kathir says in the aspect of this story:
The *karamat* (miracles done by saints) done by
these Saints are actually miracles of the Prophet
(P.B.U.H.) because they were only able to do
them through the blessing of following and
imitating the Prophet (P.B.U.H.) in all that they
did.

The Comparison between Muhammad (P.B.U.H.) and other Prophets (P.B.U.T.)

The miracles of Prophet Nuh (P.B.U.H.)

The people of Nuh (P.B.U.H.) rejected Allah's Message, they thus troubled him and gave him a hard time. He rose his hands and prayed.

Allah says:

"And Nuh (Noah) said: 'My Lord! Leave not one of the disbelievers on the earth!'"⁽¹⁾

Allah says:

"Then he invoked his Lord (saying) "I have been overcome, so help me". So we opened the gates of the Heaven with water pouring forth. And we caused springs to gush forth from the earth. So the waters (of the Heaven and earth) met for a matter predestined. And we carried him on a (ship) made of planks

181

and nails. Floating under Our Eyes: A reward for him who has been rejected. And indeed, we have left this as a sign. Then is there any that will remember (or receive admonition)?"

When Prophet Nuh (Noah) prayed, Allah answered his prayer. He sent down heavy rains that caused floods which submerged the land and mountain, the only living thing that survived was what was carried in the ship that Nuh (P.B.U.H.) built.

The same situation befell Muhammad (P.B.U.H.) in Taif, where they stoned him (P.B.U.H.) severely. Allah then sent the Angel of the Mountain and ordered them to be obedient to him. The Angle asked the Prophet whether he should destroy that town, the Prophet (P.B.U.H.) chose to be patient instead of punishing them, hoping that from their offspring there would come those who will believe in him (P.B.U.H.).

When the people of the past Prophets (P.B.U.T.) used to think of them as being incompetent and mad, the Prophets (P.B.U.T.) used to respond to such comments themselves but as for Muhammad (P.B.U.H.) it is Allah Himself who used to respond for him.

Allah the Exalted says:

"And they say. "O you (Muhammad (P.B.U.H.)) to whom the Dhikri (the Qur'an) has been sent down! Verily, you are a mad man!". "Why do you not bring angels to us if you are truthful?". We do not send the angels down except with the truth (i.e. for torment) and in that case, they (disbelievers) would have no respite".

وَقَالُواْ يَٰٓأَيُّهَا ٱلَّذِى نُزِّلَ عَلَيْهِ ٱلذِّكْرُ إِنَّكَ لَمَجْنُونٌ ۝

كَذَٰلِكَ مَآ أَتَى ٱلَّذِينَ مِن قَبْلِهِم مِّن رَّسُولٍ إِلَّا قَالُواْ سَاحِرٌ أَوْ مَجْنُونٌ ۝

The miracles of Prophet Hu'd (P.B.U.H.)

Abu Naim said: Allah the Exalted destroyed the people of Prophet Hu'd with strong winds while He saved the Prophet (P.B.U.H.) Muhammad with strong winds and dust the day of Al-Ahzab.

Allah says:

"O you who believe remember Allah's Favour to you, when there came to you hosts and we sent against them wind and forces that you saw not [troops of angels during the battle of Ahzab (the Confederates)]. And Allah is Ever All-Seer of what you do".

He said: Ibn Abbas (R.A.) narrated that on the day of Al-Ahzab the south (wind) moved together with the north and Allah saved Muhammad and sent wind and dust which chased the enemies.

وَأَقِيمُواْ ٱلصَّلَوٰةَ وَءَاتُواْ ٱلزَّكَوٰةَ وَمَا تُقَدِّمُواْ لِأَنفُسِكُم مِّنْ خَيْرٍ تَجِدُوهُ عِندَ ٱللَّهِ إِنَّ ٱللَّهَ بِمَا تَعْمَلُونَ بَصِيرٌ ۝

The miracles of Prophet Saleh (P.B.U.H.)

Abu Naim said: If it is said Prophet Saleh (P.B.U.H.) produced a camel from a rock and it was a miracle for his people. We say that Prophet Muhammad (P.B.U.H.) was given more than that. For example, the camel which complained to him about mistreatment by its owner and stones and trees that greeted him.

The miracles of Prophet Ibrahim (P.B.U.H.)

When Ibrahim (Abraham) (P.B.U.H.) was thrown in the grand fire made by King Namrod, the fire declined to burn Ibrahim (P.B.U.H.) by Allah's command.

Our Sheikh Abu Al-Maali Al-Zamkani said: Some men in the Ummah of Prophet Muhammad (P.B.U.H.) have also been thrown in fire and were never bunt too because of Allah and the blessings of our Prophet (P.B.U.H.).

He said: Al-Khulani was thrown in a fire in

185

Yemen because of his being a Muslim and the fire declined to burn him. When he came back to Medina the Prophet (P.B.U.H.) had already past away and Abu Bakr was the Caliph. Umar saw him and recognized him, he asked: Are you He who was thrown in fire and never got burnt.

He said: Yes by Allah I am the one. On hearing this Umar kissed his forehead and took him to Abu Bakr and said: Praise be to Allah He who has shown us what was done to Ibrahim (P.B.U.H.) at the time of Prophet Muhammad (P.B.U.H.).

The Clear Signs given to Prophet Musa (P.B.U.H.)

Prophet Musa (P.B.U.H.) was given many signs but the Greatest of them were nine, which are mentioned in the Qur'an:

"And indeed we gave Musa (Moses) nine clear signs. Ask them the Children of Israel, when he came to them, then Firaun

(Pharaoh) said to him: 'O Musa (Moses) I think you are indeed bewitched'".

He also divided the Red Sea and the children of Israel walked through, when Allah ordered him to do so. He prayed against the people of Pharaoh when they disbelieved in him and Allah sent them floods, locust, lice, frogs, blood and others. Musa's stick could turn to a snake and his hand bright as if it was a piece of the moon.

Prophet Muhammad (P.B.U.H.) like Musa (P.B.U.H.) was given a sign too of, the cleavage of the moon, stones used to supplicate on his hands and the rock in Mecca that used to greet him. Among his companions Alaa Ibn Al-Hadhramy (R.A.) and Abu Ubaid Al-Thaqafi (R.A.) were soldiers who used to walk on water. If no one but Musa (P.B.U.H.) spoke to the Allah directly, we say Muhammad (P.B.U.H.) spoke to

Allah directly in a place where even Jibril (Gabriel) has never reached at *Sidrat Al-Muntahah* which is above the seven skies in the night of *Miraj*. If it is said that Musa (P.B.U.H.) struck a rock with his stick and twelve fountains of water splashed out, we say Muhammed (P.B.U.H.) had a miracle just like him or more wonderous; water sprung out from his fingers. May the peace and blessings of Allah be upon all of them.

Yusha' Ibn Nun stops the sun from setting

Yusha' was a Prophet among the Prophets of the Children of Israel after Musa (P.B.U.H.). He is the one who took out the children of Israel from the wilderness and led them in to *Bait-ul-Maqdis* (Jerusalem) after a battle.

It was on Friday evening, the war was at its climax and they were almost winning but the sun was just about to set. So Yusha' stood and faced the sun and said: "Indeed you have your orders and I have mine …then he said: O Allah stop it (sun) from setting for me…" Allah stopped it from setting until they conquered their enemy, then He let it set.

Imam Ahmad relates that Abu Hurairah (R.A.) said that the Prophet (P.B.U.H.) said: "Indeed the sun has never been barred for anyone except Yusha' the night he entered *Bait-ul-Maqdis*".

What was given to both Prophet Idris (P.B.U.H.) and Muhammad (P.B.U.H.)

Abu Naim said: Prophet Idris was given a high rank.

Allah the Exalted says:

"And mention Idris (Enoch) in the Qur'an, Verily he was a man of truth (and) a Prophet. And We raised him to a high station"

The Prophet Muhammad (P.B.U.H.) was

given more than this. Ibn Jarir relates from Anas Ibn Malik that: The Prophet (P.B.U.H.) said: ...... O Lord, You have honored all the Prophets who came before me, You made Ibrahim (P.B.U.H.) your *Al-Khalil* (Allah's bosom friend) and Musa (P.B.U.H.) *Al-Kalim* (spokesman of Allah), and Daud (P.B.U.H.) you made the mountain subservient to him and You gave Prophet Sulaiman (P.B.U.H.) powers to control the wind and the Jinn, and Issa (P.B.U.H.) You gave him powers to resurrect the dead, so what have You blessed me with? He said (Allah): Did I not give you what was better than all of that? I am not mentioned without you being mentioned with me......"

$$وَإِنَّكَ لَعَلَىٰ خُلُقٍ عَظِيمٍ ﴿٤﴾$$

What was given to Prophet Daud (P.B.U.H.) was given to Prophet Muhammad (P.B.U.H.)

Allah the exalted says:

"Be patient (O Muhammad SAW) of what they say, and remember Our slave Daud (David) endued with power. Verily, he was ever oft-returning in all matters and in repentance (towards Allah). Verily, We made the mountains to glorify Our Praises with him [Daud (David)] in the As-hi (after midday till sunset) and Ishraq (from sunrise till midday)".

Allah the Exalted says:

"And indeed we bestowed grace on Daud (David) from us (saying); O you mountains. Glorify (Allah) with him! And you birds (also)! And we made the iron soft for him".

Prophet Daud (P.B.U.H.) was given a nice voice by which he praised Allah. His voice was so nice that the birds and mountains used to praise Allah with him. We have mentioned that the Prophet (P.B.U.H.) also used to be greeted by trees, and rocks and stones used to supplicate Allah on the Prophet's hands.

He used to eat from the work of his hands and so did our Prophet (P.B.U.H.). In the Sahih, Imam Al-Bukhari narrates that Ibn Mas'ud said: We used to hear the food that the Prophet (P.B.U.H.) ate praising Allah.

What was given to Prophet Issa Ibn Maryam (P.B.U.H.) and Muhammad (P.B.U.H.)

Allah created Adam (P.B.U.H.) from dust, without a father and a mother and created Hawa from a man without a woman and created Prophet Issa (P.B.U.H.) from the Word (be and he was), which was blown by Jibril to Mariam, he created him from a woman without a man.

Prophet Issa ascended to the sky just like the Prophet (P.B.U.H.) Muhammad went from Masjid Haram to Bait-ul-Maqdis then ascended to the sky.

Miracles of Prophet Issa (P.B.U.H.)

The miracles of Issa son of Mary (P.B.U.H.) were the resurrection of the dead, restoration of sight and the curing of leprosy.

Our scholar Ibn Zamlakani analyzed the miracles of the our Prophet (P.B.U.H.) as follows:-

Firstly, he resurrected a part of an animal.

Secondly, he resurrected a part of an animal separated from the rest of it.

Thirdly, he resurrected an animal, gave it back its life, brain and instincts.

O'Allah, grant us health and well-being always, in this world and in the Hereafter.

إِنَّ رَبَّكَ يَعْلَمُ أَنَّكَ تَقُومُ أَدْنَىٰ مِن ثُلُثَيِ ٱلَّيْلِ وَنِصْفَهُۥ وَثُلُثَهُۥ وَطَآئِفَةٌ مِّنَ ٱلَّذِينَ مَعَكَ وَٱللَّهُ يُقَدِّرُ ٱلَّيْلَ وَٱلنَّهَارَ عَلِمَ أَن لَّن تُحْصُوهُ فَتَابَ عَلَيْكُمْ فَٱقْرَءُوا۟ مَا تَيَسَّرَ مِنَ ٱلْقُرْءَانِ عَلِمَ أَن سَيَكُونُ مِنكُم مَّرْضَىٰ وَءَاخَرُونَ يَضْرِبُونَ فِى ٱلْأَرْضِ يَبْتَغُونَ مِن فَضْلِ ٱللَّهِ وَءَاخَرُونَ يُقَٰتِلُونَ فِى سَبِيلِ ٱللَّهِ فَٱقْرَءُوا۟ مَا تَيَسَّرَ مِنْهُ وَأَقِيمُوا۟ ٱلصَّلَوٰةَ وَءَاتُوا۟ ٱلزَّكَوٰةَ وَأَقْرِضُوا۟ ٱللَّهَ قَرْضًا حَسَنًا وَمَا تُقَدِّمُوا۟ لِأَنفُسِكُم مِّنْ خَيْرٍ تَجِدُوهُ عِندَ ٱللَّهِ هُوَ خَيْرًا وَأَعْظَمَ أَجْرًا وَٱسْتَغْفِرُوا۟ ٱللَّهَ إِنَّ ٱللَّهَ غَفُورٌ رَّحِيمٌ ۝

Indeed, your Lord knows, [O Muhammad], that you stand [in prayer] almost two thirds of the night or half of it or a third of it, and [so do] a group of those with you. And Allah determines [the extent of] the night and the day. He has known that you [Muslims] will not be able to do it and has turned to you in forgiveness, so recite what is easy [for you] of the Qur'an. He has known that there will be among you those who are ill and others traveling throughout the land seeking [something] of the bounty of Allah and others fighting for the cause of Allah . So recite what is easy from it and establish prayer and give zakah and loan Allah a goodly loan. And whatever good you put forward for yourselves - you will find it with Allah . It is better and greater in reward. And seek forgiveness of Allah . Indeed, Allah is Forgiving and Merciful.